Twayne's English Authors Series

Sylvia E. Bowman, *Editor*

INDIANA UNIVERSITY

T. H. White

T. H. White

T. H. WHITE

By JOHN K. CRANE
The Pennsylvania State University

Twayne Publishers, Inc. :: New York

Library of Congress Cataloging in Publication Data

Crane, John K
T. H. White.

(Twayne's English authors series, TEAS 172)
Bibliography: p. 195.

1. White, Terence Hanbury, 1906–1964—Criticism and interpretation.
PR6045.H2Z6 828'.9'1209 74-4121
ISBN 0–8057–1573–8

MANUFACTURED IN THE UNITED STATES OF AMERICA

This book is for

Marge and Kenneth and Scott

with love

Contents

About the Author

Preface

Chronology

1. Not of This Life and of It 17

2. A Gray White 22

3. The Years Before Arthur 52

4. *The Once and Future King* 75

5. The Neoclassicist 123

6. The Last Ten Years 163

Conclusion 186

Notes and References 189

Selected Bibliography 195

Index 199

About the Author

John K. Crane is Associate Professor of English at The Pennsylvania State University where he teaches courses in Modern and Medieval Literature. He received his Ph.D. from Penn State in 1966; and, before returning there in 1971 in his current capacity, he was Assistant Professor of English at the United States Air Force Academy and the University of Southern California. He also served as Lecturer in Linguistics at the University of Colorado, Colorado Springs, between 1967 and 1969, and as Visiting Professor of Modern Literature at the University of Washington in the summer of 1970.

Professor Crane has published numerous articles on the *Gawain-Poet*, Faulkner, Golding, *Beowulf*, and Chaucer. He is preparing a book dealing with the manifestations of Determinism in British Literature between 1880 and 1930, which includes studies of Hardy, Conrad, Gissing, Moore, Shaw, Joyce, Maugham, Yeats, Lawrence, and other writers of the age. During the period 1967–1971, Professor Crane was a Contributor to the Bibliography of the Modern Language Association of America and during the last two years served as the Bibliographer in charge of American Imprints.

Professor Crane is active in the MLA and the Modern Humanities Research Association. In 1969 he served as Faculty Exchange Director for the Annual MLA Meeting. He has been a Section Chairman at several professional meetings and has served as consultant for a number of publishers on various scholarly books.

Preface

Today, a preface to a book on T. H. White need hardly justify it nor apologize for its existence. White is a writer whom nearly everyone admires but whom scholars continue to neglect. Recently (1967), Sylvia Warner opened White scholarship with a brilliant biography of the man so few knew or understood. The following year, White's close friend David Garnett released in book form the letters which constitute their twenty-eight-year correspondence, letters which nicely supplement the biography. But nothing has yet appeared on the two dozen books which made T. H. White a writer of international importance. There have been two or three small articles in scholarly journals and a eulogy in *Time* magazine, but little else has appeared. The present book is intended, therefore, to offset this omission.

I have attempted to provide a substantial examination of each work and have tried, as well, to remain entirely objective in the appraisal of each. White, himself, nurtures objectivity, for he can be so fine an artist at one moment and so clumsy and tedious at another. Luckily for his readers, this distinction is most evident between two books rather than between two passages within one. Perhaps the most crucial objective of this volume, though, is the *proper* establishment of White's literary merit, for the works by him that have so far received wide recognition are generally appreciated for less-than-the-best reasons. A Walt Disneyish aura still surrounds *The Sword and the Stone*, for example, even though the book itself is so much more than the things the cartoon version chose to emphasize. *The Goshawk* is not the book on falconry that so many library catalogues call it—it is close to being a poetic study in Romantic metaphysics. *The Godstone and the Blackymor* is a reflection on White's own process of humanization; certainly Irish folklore is not its primary, or even secondary, concern.

I have divided the works into what seem to me to be five distinct periods—the search for the correct form of expression, the mature years when the first important work began to appear, the Arthurian years when White was assuring his place in English literature, the scholarly years which momentarily diverted White from his talent as a novelist into the pursuits of satirist and essayist, and the final years, years of uneven achievement and declining powers. Because so many of White's lesser books are so difficult to obtain today, I have tried, when possible, to present quotations which convey the flavor (and White *is* a "flavor" writer) of his work. Due to his extensive production and the limited space available for this study, this book is more general and at times more superficial than it would like to be—perhaps, hopefully, others will be quickly along with more detailed analyses of the more important work.

Most lists of acknowledgments begin by acknowledging the impossibility of acknowledging those deserving to be acknowledged. I suppose it *is* impossible, but an author should at least try. First, I am grateful to the officials of the following publishers for allowing me to use portions of their books: Chatto and Windus, W. Heffer and Sons, Cassell, Viking Press, Alfred A. Knopf, G. P. Putnam's Sons, William Collins Sons, and Jonathan Cape. I appreciate the courtesy with which the following libraries made books available:: The Library of Congress, Harvard University Library, the University of Colorado Libraries, and the United States Air Force Academy Library. For an author so profuse as T. H. White, older books are bound to be hard to find; the following people were invaluable in uncovering things which would have otherwise remained buried: Mrs. Betty Fogler, United States Air Force Academy Library; Valerie Kettley and Mr. E. M. Barrett of Jonathan Cape, London; and especially Mrs. Norah Smallwood of Chatto and Windus and Miss Penelope Springett of Collins, both of London.

Other who were set to running down impossible items (because of their unfortunate geographical locations at the moment various whims hit me) were Professors Richard J. Dunn of the University of Washington, Gerald B. Kinneavy of the University of Colorado, and Frank Brady of the City University of New York, Miss Marilyn Eitman of Putnam's, and my father, Mr. John P. Crane of Stamford, Connecticut. Those who provided invaluable insights into the man T. H. White, insights without which this book would have been very bare, were Sylvia Townsend Warner, David Garnett, Professor William M. Murphy of Union College, and the Reverend Mark J. Hunt of the Theology Department of Iona College.

Special gratitude is due as well to my typist, Mrs. Rose Maruska of Colorado Springs, who labored cheerfully while enduring various unwarranted pressures. In attempting to thank everyone, I am sure I have invariably neglected someone—to him, I apologize.

I will not forget my wife and sons, however, whom I thank for putting up with me through it all, and to whom this book is lovingly dedicated.

JOHN K. CRANE

University Park, Pennsylvania

Chronology

1906 T. H. White born May 29, Bombay, India, only child of Garrick White, a district superintendent of police, and Constance Aston White, daughter of an Indian judge.

1911 White brought to England by his parents to live at St. Leonard's.

1920 White attends Cheltenham College; lives with the Astons while his bickering parents live in India.

1922 C. F. Scott points out White's literary talent to him and becomes, according to White, the most important influence in his life.

1923 White's parents, after years of discord, obtain a divorce.

1925 Enters Cambridge University, where he is tutored by L. J. Potts, henceforth to be his lifelong friend.

1927 Discovers he has tuberculosis, initially diagnosed as terminal. Spends four months in a sanatorium.

1928 In Italy for his health; begins draft of his first piece of creative literature, *They Winter Abroad,* though several other books were eventually to see print before this one. He also contracts with Chatto and Windus for "a book of poems," and writes several articles for the *Saturday Review.*

1929 White's first book, *Loved Helen and Other Poems,* published in England by Chatto and Windus and in America by Viking Press. *The Green Bay Tree; or Wicked Man Touches Wood* is issued by Heffer in its series of Cambridge poets called "Songs for Sixpence." Graduates from Cambridge with Distinction.

1930 Becomes assistant master at a preparatory school in southern England. Through 1932, this is the helter-skelter period of composition in which White was working on five books at once.

1931 *Dead Mr. Nixon,* written in collaboration with R. McNair Scott.

1932 Publication of *Darkness at Pemberley. They Winter Abroad* and *First Lesson* published under the pseudonym "James Aston." White is fired from the preparatory school; becomes head of the English Department at Stowe in the fall.

1933 *Farewell Victoria.* He acquires Brownie at Tingewick during the Christmas Holidays.

1934 *Earth Stopped.*

1935 *Gone to Ground.* White temporarily blinded in an automobile accident, March 1.

1936 *England Have My Bones.* White begins treatment for the curing of his homosexuality. He resigns his position at Stowe to devote full time to writing. In January of this year, his friendship with David Garnett commences. He also keeps the daybook eventually to become *The Goshawk.*

1938 *Burke's Steerage.* His friendship with Sidney Cockerell and his interest in the Roxburgh Bestiary both begin in this year. Late in this year, *The Sword in the Stone* is published; beginning of White's financial independence.

1939 *The Witch in the Wood* (later titled *The Queen of Air and Darkness*). White begins his six-year residence in Ireland.

1940 *The Ill-Made Knight.* White abandons his intent to convert to Catholicism. His creative powers begin to succumb to the terrors of war.

1941 Writes the fifth book of the Arthurian series, "The Book of Merlyn," but it is rejected and never published.

1944 November 25–Brownie dies while White is in Dublin.

1945 White returns to England; takes up residence at Duke Mary's.

1946 *Mistress Masham's Repose.* His father dies. He takes up his final residence on the Channel Island of Alderney to escape the income taxes of England and America.

1947 *The Elephant and the Kangaroo.*

1950 *The Age of Scandal.*

1951 *The Goshawk.*

1952 *The Scandalmonger.* His mother dies in December of coronary thrombosis.

1954 *The Bestiary: A Book of Beasts*, after fifteen years in the making, is finally published.

1957 *The Master.* The summer of this year also marks the commencement of his homosexual attraction to the young boy called "Zed," an attraction which ruined his last years psychologically.

1958 *The Once and Future King* first appears as one entity, including the heretofore unpublished novel, *The Candle in the Wind.*

1959 *The Godstone and the Blackymor* (American edition is entitled *A Western Wind*). White contracts with Lerner and Loewe for the production of *Camelot.*

1962 Living in Italy.

1963 White contracts for an American lecture tour; Carol Walton travels with him as his secretary.

1964 On a Mediterranean cruise, he dies of a heart attack aboard ship in the port of Piraeus (Athens), January 17. Buried in Athens near Hadrian's Arch, January 20.

1965 *America at Last*, the journal of White's American tour, is published in the United States.

CHAPTER 1

Not of This Life and of It

"Hawks neither band themselves together in war, nor yet retire from the world of air."
Diary of T. H. White, April 26, 1939

AS a man, but not as a writer, T. H. White may be best compared to Ernest Hemingway. They were more than contemporaries and look-alikes;[1] they were also remarkably close in psychological orientation. Both were big, handsome men, each extremely vital in his approach to life. Yet each was haunted by the very talent he possessed—frightened of not only sudden death but the failure of his powers through the onslaught of age. Both were fatalists, not at all sure that the masses of humanity weren't tacitly trying to destroy each other and that God wasn't in on it all behind the scenes. Both were afraid of war, though both (White not as much as Hemingway) felt they had to participate to demonstrate their ability to deal with reality despite its horrifying definition. As substitutes for the conflict and challenges of war and life, both substituted the conflict and challenge of sport—each felt that sport was a miniature battleground in which man had a chance to test himself for the bigger fight ahead. Each had consistent need to prove himself the better of the opposition and the fear that life seemed to mount against him, and each was furious when he failed to meet the test.[2] Each failed to meet the test much more obviously with the coming of his forties and fifties, and both died premature deaths couched in unshakeable despair.

I *A Sad Existence*

T. H. White, born in India in 1906, died in Athens in 1964. In between, despite an existence of the utmost sadness, he published two dozen books "loving and praising this life."[3] White liked to compare himself to the hawk mentioned in the epigraph to this chapter, for he was a full-fledged resident of life despite the horror he discovered around him. Much has rightly been made of White's "sad existence" by Sylvia Warner,[4] David Garnett,[5] White himself, and others; and its components defy ordering. His childhood was spent amidst the bickerings of his parents and the flagellation at the Cheltenham military school—thus he grew up to be something approaching a sado-masochist, a trait he recognized, deplored, and kept amazingly well in check.

He was, by his own admission, a homosexual as well. This perversion seems to have its roots both in the behavior he observed at Cheltenham and in his mother's attempt to force all love within him toward herself. When she no longer required his constant attention, he had no place to go with the love he had to give, for "she managed to bitch up my loving women."[6] But White also kept fantastic chains upon this homosexuality. He received psychiatric help in 1936, kept it in check for twenty years, but fell in love with a young boy, Zed, in the last seven years of his life. Because he would not pervert the boy, who never understood his feelings, White's final years verged constantly on emotional explosion. During the intervening twenty years, however, he "solved" his problem through drink and through a fantastically loving devotion to his setter bitch, Brownie. Brownie, in the long run, was probably the only thing White ever had which made him really happy. When she died in 1944, the author prepared for and endured twenty years of sheer misery.

White could not exactly be called misanthropic, but his love and his respect for mankind were closely guarded. This self-protection was due mainly to the constant threat or actuality of war during the second half of his life. He one day discovered that only men and ants make war upon one another, and he was shocked at the way men of the 1930's, 1940's, and 1950's followed blindly into battle because leaders, haranguing on national patriotism, baited them to it. White's masterpiece, *The Once and Future King,* is, ultimately, an examination of mankind's addiction to warfare and of his moral and physical destruction by it. Moreover, he could never reconcile the fact that he, as a taxpayer, was forced by a faceless government (two of them for a while[7]) to make such wars possible. War as a concept was another of the great sadnesses of his life—it is interesting to note that, during World War II, he produced no work of literature.

Nonetheless, White approached life with a robust vitality, trying like the hawk to remain in the air without mixing with those who fought in it. But this vitality—in addition to being surrounded by his mother, homosexuality, war, and insensitive human beings—was hampered occasionally by serious sickness. He had tuberculosis as a young man, was partially blind in his middle years, and had heart trouble in the later ones. Of this affliction he eventually died. He drank continuously, though he had no real love for liquor—but it numbed his mind. He had, because of all this difficulty, a severe inferiority complex, which produced nauseating self-pity at one moment and unrestrained braggadoccio at another.

II *A Learner*

Yet White managed to avoid ever considering suicide, something Hemingway was not himself above. The reason, given White's peculiar psyche, is relatively easy to explain. He was a firm believer in the statement he has Merlyn make in *The Sword in the Stone* that the best thing for being sad was learning something.[8] So White learned things which were huge and diverse. In the "Pleasures of Learning" lecture that he gave many times in America in 1963, he liked to catalogue the things he had attempted in order to relieve the sadness and fear which dominated his life. Shooting a bow and arrow, flying airplanes, plowing with horses, riding show jumpers, training falcons, deep-sea diving, sailing, swimming, shooting, fishing, racing cars, throwing darts, painting, carpentering, knitting, translating, and writing are just a few. Almost all of these, of course, appear in his writings at one point or another.

Much of his melancholy was also relieved by caring for people in more difficulty than he—one of the most beautiful passages in the Warner biography concerns his attention to the deaf and blind at his Alderney home.[9] Having no regular human companionship, he vented much of his misery through letter-writing, mainly to his three closest friends (closer when they were apart than together) David Garnett, L. J. Potts, and Sidney Cockerell.[10] Often White was compelled to change residences simply to attempt a new outlook upon a life he had not yet learned to master.

After graduating from Cambridge in 1929, White spent two years as assistant master at a preparatory school but left (or was fired) because of his leniency in dealing with a homosexual affair betweeen two boys in the school. He spent the next four years (1932–36) as head of the English Department at Stowe, a position from which he eventually resigned because of the furor over several of his racier novels. From 1936 on, never again to be employed as anything other than a writer, he resided for three years in Stowe Ridings (the scene of his falconry and piloting[11]), six in Ireland (a portion of which was spent in the area of Belmullet tracing Irish fairy lore), and, after the war, one in England at Garnett's Duke Mary's. At this point, White's success as a writer was forcing him to pay taxes to two countries, a fact he both pragmatically and idealistically could not endure; and so, in 1946, he assumed his final place of residence on the Channel Island of Alderney, where, for some reason unknown even to White, the residents are exempt from income tax.

In all these "homes" White had no friends except the animals he loved: the dogs (all setter bitches, Brownie, Killie, and Jenny, successively), the hawks (Gos and Cully), an owl (Archimedes), and an assortment of other fish and fowl. In his later years the deaf and blind people to whom he attached himself came for a few weeks each summer to Alderney; and Zed, of course, was around as well. Traditionally, however, White shunned human contact. When in the 1960's he ran for a while with Julie Andrews, Richard Burton, and the *Camelot* crowd, he was obviously out of place.[12]

III *Novelist and Diarist*

White cannot be classified as a modern British writer in terms of his total literary production. The few early novels that he attempted—*They Winter Abroad, First Lesson, Earth Stopped,* and *Gone to Ground* were in the style and substance of modern British literature but were duds and flops. He was better when reverting to the style and the material of an earlier day; therefore, his best work grounds itself in the medieval era (*The Once and Future King, The Book of Beasts*), the eighteenth century (*Mistress Masham's Repose, The Age of Scandal, The Scandalmonger*), the nineteenth century (*Farewell Victoria*), or the timeless history of Irish Mythology (*The Elephant and the Kangaroo, The Godstone and the Blackymor*). In each of these ages, his imagination manages to "improve" and extend what he felt contemporary authors had left undone. White's poetry (*Loved Helen and Other Poems, The Green Bay Tree*) also smacks of an earlier day, but it is imitation rather than an extension or improvement.

Not White's greatest works but certainly his most distinctive and in some ways his most memorable are the diaries he published in book form from time to time. These provide the best picture of the author himself and the peculiar blend of enthusiasm for and fear of existence so especially characteristic of him. *England Have My Bones, The Goshawk, The Godstone and the Blackymor,* and *America at Last* are perhaps White's most flawless and realistic books.

This brief investigation of White's life is no more than a meager attempt to impose a pattern upon a life that, like the lives of all active men, is essentially patternless. The rest of this book is concerned mainly with the man's work; for a discussion of his life, Sylvia Warner's biography is unlikely to be challenged.

CHAPTER 2

A Gray White

I Loved Helen and Other Poems

T. H. WHITE'S first book, a volume of poetry entitled *Loved Helen and other Poems* (1929), contained, ironically, a Latin dedication to his mother, Constance White, the woman whose remembrance was so clearly to dominate and often to ruin much of his later work. He refers to her as first and last in his life, as the guiding principle in it, and as the source of all his happiness. He asks her to accept the book, for without her it would not have been. From what we know of the rest of White's life, there can be little more meaning in these statements than the excitement of a young author who has finally had his first manuscript accepted by a publisher. Publication was in March, 1929, and it became the poetry selection of the month for the Book Society.

The collection is divided into four sections, the second of which, consisting of ten poems, gives the work its title. The first part is entitled "First Verses" (ten poems); the third, "To Peace and Rule" (eleven poems); the last, simply "Other Poems" (ten poems). There are several pages of notes at the back of the book, though none is written by White; all are quoted directly from the sources from which he garnered his material—from the Bible to Shakespeare to Lytton Strachey.

In the section entitled "Loved Helen" there are ten poems which more gravitate together than form a unified thematic whole. There seems to be some vague reference to the Helen of Troy and Paris love affair, but this subject is in the long run inconsequential to the art of these poems. Moreover, it is also difficult to determine from poem to poem whether Helen is meant to be one particular woman or the principle of love itself. For those who have read much White before coming upon these poems, the tone and content seem strange and atypical, especially since romantic love is almost totally absent from his fiction. If the poems are personal, as surely they seem to be, there might be a very early indication in them of part of the reason for White's neglect of love both in real life and in his art. The most consistent theme in the "Loved Helen" poems is either a Keatsian fear that the beauty of love is unattainable for more than a second in time or that love is something which never *can* be truly realized.

There is no progressive order to the poems in this section, so the reader is continually shifting between White's having and not having Helen. The poems written about his actual possession are better, but they contain the pessimism and sense of transitoriness that the nonpossession poems do. Perhaps the best and most characteristic is "Thought, The Father of Pain" in which the poet expresses the persistent dread that the head or mind will eventually defeat the heart and deprive it of its emotional rapture. After asking Helen, almost rhetorically, whether their rapture can be prolonged, he proceeds to answer himself negatively, employing the dominant metaphor of an adder to emphasize his denial:

> In a year my mind's adder
> Will be seven skins more old,
> Seven skins wiser and sadder,
> Dafter, re-sold. (17)[1]

The mind takes the natural course of love and infects it with a jealous hatred, which in turn eliminates the rapture and returns the love affair to its original state of neutrality:

> No links or soft regrets: We shall be parted
> Two years in time, otherwise just the same.
> I shall be as tired as when I started,
> You as indifferent as before you knew my name. (17–18)

This particular poem, unlike some of the others, offers a tenuous solution, one about which he is skeptical at best:

But if speculation
Can be induced to sleep
Somewhere, somehow, we might still keep
Safe a less deep relation.
We might still hold a mutual benefit
Of help and comfort, trust,
Almost physical but less than lust:
Not always jealous to love but pleased to sit
Knee to knee, by firesides, sound and sure. (18)

This attribution of the difficulties of love to a mind which tries to rationalize its lust is not consistent throughout the poems. Rather, the lover's main problem seems to be one of assuming that what he has cannot possibly last; therefore, he rationalizes it into a state of secondary importance and fabricates alternatives when the love is gone. The poems become almost restatements of Prufrockian innocence. In "If I Can Remember," the poet tries to tell Helen (but more so himself) that just the memory of her will suffice once she has deserted him. He concludes this poem by saying "I should in short be a very blessed creature" (20) if he should be permitted this recollection; but the tone again is one of unintentional defensiveness in preparation for the moment that his intellect tells him will surely come.

In the short poem "Interim," he refers to love as "the mad folk's holiday" (21) amidst the "jealousy and hate and obstinacy and pride" (21) that the mind imposes upon the love affair, implying that the mind always rules the heart, forcing men and women to be more unnatural than natural. This implication, however, seems to be a scientific analysis of an impending catastrophe. One of the better poems of the group is "Blood of the Nightingale" which seems to be an answer to an apparent admonition by Helen to stop being so pessimistic about their chances for a happy future. The poem is somewhat different from the others because it invokes a note of hope with which to calm her oncoming despair:

We shall know
Beauty
With a quieter and newer security
After the shady valley. (24)

This sentiment, of course, is rather archaic, but it is about as positive as the "Loved Helen" poems ever become; at least, it is the only poem that envisions a purposeful future in the relationship with Helen. "Home" is a short poem which suddenly solves all the difficulties expressed by the first nine, but with the same method of equivocation that characterizes the poet throughout these poems. The first line ("Out of love, out of lust, we are safest now" [26]), sets the tone of relief, and the second line ("The dregs are not bitter as they said they would be" [26]) reinforces it, at least for the poet. The remainder is standard stoicism until a rather surprising final two lines in which the trumped-up tone of relief and happiness is shattered by a deterministic statement about human existence. Being finally apart, the lovers will sing long:

> And from dawn to darkness down the years
> Find dawn and darkness. We are home. (26)

The Helen poems, then, are the product of a poet who is concealing his true emotions behind pat solutions and stoicism, and we have the distinct feeling that the solutions and stoicism are supposed to be taken at face value. Some of the poems are rhythmical and easy reading; but others, such as the opening one entitled "Lost," are overly burdened with strained imagery and strained meter:

> If one day down my iron avenues
> The tubes and cubes, leading, at last, me right,
> Should lose their remorseless patterns and diffuse,
> Into a kinder symmetry, and shew me how
> After a white hand pointing Exit, shine the stars at night: . . . (15)

White is trying too hard to emulate the modern poetic stylists and is not being the traditionalist that his other poetry and future fiction certify him to be. "Lost," a statement of the poet's confusion and lack of identity due to the nonpossession of Helen, serves as a poor and misleading introduction to the other nine poems, ones more concrete and pointed in their technique.

The "Loved Helen" section contains a variety of rhyme

schemes and metrical patterns, so much so that it is impossible to center upon a dominant motif. Often he will go as far as five lines into the poem to complete a rhyme (*abccba*), and at other times four rhymes run concurrently (*abcdabcd*). While the experimentation is interesting, the radical departure from more standard rhyme schemes leads us into temporarily believing we are reading blank verse. The variation and originality, though, are invigorating for a while.

The first group of poems in the volume, those called "First Verses," have "Death" as their central subject and vary greatly in quality, though the experimentation is still present. The volume's opening poem, "After Continual Defeat," is an Italian sonnet with a variant rhyme scheme. This poem, one of the more memorable in this collection, states simply the desire either to be shown the purpose of life or to be told, pointblank, that there is none—but, in any event, to be allowed to stop guessing. This poem is followed by two more sonnets on death, the second of which ("From the Dead World") is a very Romantic, mythological, semi-Christian vision of Heaven as a place of ultimate joy until the last line where the skeptical poet reveals "I'd like to think this true" (5). The most interesting aspect of this particular poem is the contrast to it that White draws in the one which follows, for he takes the opening line and a half from the first poem and affixes it, minus a comma, to the second, entitled "Consumptive." This poem is a direct rebuttal and reversal of the one preceding:

From the dead world he died [,] and wheeled away
Into the abyss of life: there beamed his light,
The Bishop said, in everlasting day.
But I, whose only eyes held no long sight,
Saw the less spiritual wrong where he saw right.
Focussed the boy, his cheeks were bright,
Whose golden hair grew dark and later grey;
His eyes I saw, caught like a child's by night.
I watched when, death bespoken, in that coil
He beat about for God, misfound, and came to die
Rod-kissed. His red and shredded life at last with toil
He coughed: and while the Bishop ranged his keener eye
I saw him taken to a mortuary.

This fourth poem in the book is the fourth one about death, and it is also almost the fourth sonnet, but it stops one line short. The effect White gains by omitting one line is to have something seem to be missing—just as something in the human experience seems to be for the poet who has weighed and evaluated several interpretations of human destiny and death. The next poem, "Peace on Earth," reveals White avoiding the sonnet form altogether, though Death and the thought that it is pleasanter not to have any reason to hope for a God than to hope without reason are still very obvious. This point, in fact, seems to me to be the guiding principle of the entire volume of poetry: that earthly illusion is the germ of tragedy; and, the sooner man realizes it is so, the happier he will be. The opening poems present bluntly the poet's attitude toward death, and later ones are equally direct about the value of earthly love.

The next two poems in "First Verses," "Lament" (which places the poet's life at the end of a chain of great and beautiful people who have met death) and "Conversazione" (a rather trite statement of the finality death brings despite the love of life the poet might have), lack either the quality or the originality of the opening ones. "Station" contains a semieffective metaphor, which almost approaches the level of a conceit; it compares a train and a tunnel to a coffin and a tomb, each taking away loved ones. The mourner and the person left on the platform feel equally helpless about how to continue. "Pharaoh" is relatively standard death poetry, resembling to a great degree Shelley's "Ozymandias." The last poem of this set, entitled "Atlas," is a statement, directly addressed by the poet to his love, which points out that earthly love in the face of death is no more helpful than the nonappearing Hercules for whom Atlas waited in classical mythology. This poem is the transition, somewhat effectively but not totally so, for the "Loved Helen" poems which follow.

In the third section, "To Peace and Rule and Other Poems," the themes are not so consistent as the title would seem to indicate; but death is still very much present. All told, the poems in this section are more metaphysical; more interested in first principles and in various interpretations of divine power than those of the first two sections; they are also generally longer. At no point in his career was White perfectly at home with scholarly material, and he certainly is not here; for the poetry is not nearly so lucid or so meaningful amid the clutter of Buddha, Ananda, and Christ. In several of the poems, however, he seems to be imitating his favorite poets; for we find occasional hints of T. S. Eliot, Dylan Thomas, Walt Whitman, and Yeats. Perhaps the most noticeable are the very Hopkinsian lines in "No Alchemy":

> The untold gold fool found where wiseman missed,
> Fool-found, and passed by fool with empty eyes.
> Turn lead to gold? Much rather gold to lead:
> Touch it, like fool, and the old gold is dead,
> Dross. (43)

The poem is about the ability of the human senses to experience the beauty of the world, and it is one of the few in which White's poetry does not seem strained for the occasion in this volume.

The volume's weakest poems are in the final section, "Other Poems," an easy-out, catch-all which ropes in diverse, random topics, many of which are beyond the young White's ability to communicate. In one way or another, all seem to deal with Time, but only the one entitled "Grace" approaches in merit the volume's earlier verses. The crucial defect in the final poems is excessive sentimentality.

White's attempts to be a poet are mostly early in his career which may or may not have been fortunate; for, while he surely has poetic talent, it does not seem to me to be varied enough or, in the long run, original and substantial enough to make him a poet of any ultimate importance. Poetry does not seem to be the form for either his peculiar sense of humor or his raised-eyebrow approach to life. His verse becomes more sentimental, more sensuous than White the man himself really is. *Loved Helen and Other Poems* contains some good poetry, but none that even approaches greatness; and not much of the real T. H. White appears through the guarded and defensive tone. But then, this will, for some time to come, also be true of his fiction.[2]

II *"The Green Bay Tree"*

White's second published work was a poem entitled "The Green Bay Tree; or, The Wicked Man Touches Wood," which covered only two printed pages and was bound in a paper cover. It is clearly modeled upon the work of Gerard Manley Hopkins, one of White's favorite poets.[3] Some two years later White even ventured upon a critical study of Hopkins's poetry, a book he abandoned after a "first joyous chapter of demolishing previous critics."[4] From the first line, "From wood, the virtue sap, life thread, hold power by touch:," the heavily accented, overly economical sprung rhythm of the Jesuit is continuously present. In reading this line, we cannot help recalling the famous line from "Carrion Comfort" which reads "Can something, hope, wish day come, not choose not to be" or another in the same poem "... why wouldst thou rude on me / Thy wring-world right foot rock."[5] Alliteration, assonance, and consonance are also present in most lines of "The Green Bay Tree"; the following couplet is an example:

> We have broken continuity, are plucked to clutch
> At straws by waves, by waves are plucked and tossed.

Even beyond the technical devices of a Hopkins poem, the subject matter, that of spiritual agony tempered by persistent hope, is also, with necessary modifications of religious outlook, the theme of this poem.

The poem, thirty-three lines long, is divided into three sections: the first states the problem of man cut spiritually adrift in the material world, the second gives the poet's reasons why the problem exists, and the third attempts a solution.

The first part, consisting of thirteen lines in two stanzas, establishes "wood" as the undefined but most positive symbol in the poem. Wood is probably a representation of either Nature, in a semi-Wordsworthian sense, or, more generally, the natural strength which, though inherent in man, is often overlooked or misused. Among other things, wood is referred to as "the virtue sap," "life thread," the core of benevolence, and "bather's rope ... for eventing gales." Wood functions all through the poem as a practical material product and as a symbol of spiritual strength. It is significant that the symbol of such strength is wood and not steel or iron; for the poet, things made of wood "Hold power, but not too much." This deliberate weakening of the symbol is anomalous here, but is repeated and clarified later in the poem.

The second stanza of the first part makes no reference to the introductory stanza. It speaks of man's *hubris* and indiscretion which have separated him from the continuity of natural life and placed him at the mercy of Saturn and limbo. The dominant image is the sea, and it seems here to symbolize eternity. In this sea is mankind who is clutching "At straws by waves, by waves [is] plucked and tossed." Man has set foot upon the shores of Time and has been swept out into a chaotic and uncertain sea. Helplessly, he clutches for a rope ("raw wet hemp," a product of wood) to pull himself back; but his effort is hopeless.

The opening line of the second part (fourteen lines, two stanzas) is identical to the initial line of the first part—once again identifying wood as the symbol of limited strength and continuity. In the first stanza of this section, White obliquely accuses man of excessive pride (*hubris*) in assuming that he has the strength to tackle the sea (eternity). Water eventually rots wood (man's limited strength) and sinks it (in desperation):

> Return, take purpose, leave the unlimited deep.
> Strike out no more, we are not built for oceans.

And the succeeding two lines make clear why we are not so built:

> The Atlantic closes on the beating arm and falls asleep.
> The pond Pacific need not wake to drown us.

The strains of determinism are clear, as is the fact that seeking beyond the immediate human experience is both a lethargic and insignificant pursuit (pond Pacific). In short, there is no positive value in eternity, since no life after death is anywhere in evidence. The sea (eternity) is thus nothing more than a "vacuum" which smooths over the dead.

Part III is White's guardedly positive alternative—his solution. Where Hopkins recommends forsaking the earth in favor of the eternal, White does the opposite: he tells man to abandon the proud purposes of immortality and be dragged back to shore on the wood-made rope (for which he was fumbling in Part I). He orders recognition of both the potentialities and limitations of human life; and, having so recognized them, "Live, go on, conquer, love, flourish, and rest." The rest is permanent and mortal—exactly, White feels, what one who has lived, gone on, conquered, loved, and flourished is entitled to have.

The poem is not a bad piece of work; but it suffers from too much imitation of style and tone, both of which, since the outcome and the substance of the poem are so different from Hopkins, turn it into almost an intentional parody. However, just like much of Hopkins's own poetry, the solution, though positive and credible, is also guarded and restrained. It lacks, for both the poet and the audience, the certainty which the very nature of the unknowable prohibits.

III Dead Mr. Nixon

From poetry, White, still seeking a medium, turned to detective stories. *Dead Mr. Nixon* was written in 1931 in collaboration with his friend R. McNair Scott while White was concurrently composing *Darkness at Pemberley, Farewell Victoria*, and *First Lesson*. The bulk of the work seems to be Scott's, though exactly how much is not certain. Sylvia Warner tells us that White wrote the opening chapters and the wild finale, but she makes no estimate about exactly where White's work begins and ends.[6] The prose style in the middle of the book (presumably Scott's since it does not resemble anything else of White's) is extremely paratactic. Chapters 1, 2, and 3 and chapters 19, 20, 21, and 22, the last four, seem more to resemble White's flowing hypotaxis—thus, it would seem that he is responsible for only about one-third of the entire composition. How much of the idea is his is impossible to estimate, but *Darkness at Pemberley* demonstrates his own ability to write complexly plotted mysteries.

Dead Mr. Nixon, very unlike White's later work, is full of attempted and successful murders; it is always exciting reading, but not particularly good from a literary standpoint. The plot—and the book is almost all plot—is cleverly conceived, though it becomes progressively harder to credit as the story progresses. Most of the characters are two dimensional, with the exception of Mr. Nixon (a secondary character to whom some catharsis seems supposed to be attached) who is even more poorly drawn. Universal or metaphysical insights to be found in *Dead Mr. Nixon* are, thus, pretty thoroughly obscured.

We are faced at the outset with deciding whether, since this was the first novel to which White attached his name, it was intended merely as quick-sale sensationalism or whether some artistic purpose was intended which never materialized. The tale opens with two sudden and violent murders, neither of which happens in accord with the perpetrator's plans. In the first, the Wimble family of Worcestershire, while entertaining Mr. Hurley—its American guest—on a bird shoot, is fired upon from a nearby road by two men who are armed with a machine gun. Hurley, the intended victim, is just grazed; but his valet falls dead. In Chapter 2, the scene shifts without transition to the boardinghouse in which a college professor named Adrian Nycher lives. Nycher is in the process of being blackmailed by his landlady over an incriminatory letter she has discovered; and, seeing his hard-earned career about to be ruined, he plans to murder her.

Despite elaborate preparations which ensure that he will never be tied to the crime, he kills her while her lover is lying under her bed. After Nycher has been recognized and has to change his identity, the novel follows Nycher to Scotland, where he is picked up by a former friend named Spektor and taken to the home of Spektor's boss (a defrocked priest who now surrounds himself with criminals whose security he guarantees in return for their bodily protection of him). As it turns out, the priest, named Stiles, was the brains behind the attempt on the life of Hurley; for Stiles, who had more or less raped Hurley's daughter (after which she died in childbirth), knew that Hurley had come to England to murder him. Stiles, irritated because his own henchmen have bungled the job, threatens to turn Nycher (who now calls himself Nixon) in to the police if he will not cooperate; and he devises a plan by which Spektor, a business acquaintance of Hurley's, will lure the American to what is supposedly Nixon's flat in London for the purpose of examining a plant model in which Hurley's interest could be generated. When Hurley discovers that Nixon is a fake, he will leave and walk out the door into a trap to be sprung by the remaining two henchmen.

The plan works smoothly until, leaving the building, Hurley (whose life has already been threatened in the past few days) becomes suspicious and gives his hat and coat to a janitor. The janitor, leaving the front door dressed like Hurley, is gunned down. The story becomes even more complex at this point, because Spektor, who has no love for Father Stiles, is interested in Hurley's death for another reason—stock speculation in Hurley's company. His plan is to sell thousands of shares of stock (which he does not yet own) in Hurley's business for five pounds a share and, after the agreement is made, reveal to the market that Hurley is dead and that his business was based on bootlegging (which is true), and then buy the necessary amount of shares from present holders at only fifteen shillings apiece and sell them at five pounds to the buyers whom he has already contracted. When Spektor realizes several hours after this second attempt on Hurley's life that it was a failure, he himself tries to kill the man in a nightclub that very night. When he fails, Spektor returns to Scotland a frightened man, knowing that, since he does not own the shares he agreed to sell for five pounds, it will cost him a good deal more to purchase enough so long as Hurley lives. Moreover, the profits he hoped to gain were to be used to extricate (by flight) himself and another of Stiles's captives (a woman named Mary) from the priest's hold.

In the midst of all this skullduggery are Margaret Wimble and Snap Thirston, two young people who want desperately to marry and will, providing that Snap can make the necessary money to satisfy Margaret's father that he is able to support her. Snap invests his entire savings in Hurley's business; and, when Hurley reveals what will happen if he is killed, Snap, Margaret, and her father become devoted to keeping him alive. The crucial period is ten days, for this would be as long as Spektor would have to make good his sales of stock. If Hurley stayed alive this amount of time, Spektor would be imprisoned for swindling. Not knowing where Stiles and Spektor reside, the Hurley side goes into hiding in an old estate in Scotland which chances to be almost just around the corner from Stiles's base of operations. In a fantastic and totally incredible scene, Stiles, Spektor, Nixon, and sixteen henchmen gun their way into Hurley's hideaway, indispose (including kill) several of his friends, and kidnap him.

Returned to Stiles's place, Spektor (since this is the ninth day) wants to kill Hurley immediately but discovers that the gruesome Stiles knows his plan to desert. Stiles places Hurley under Nixon's watch (both to spite the miserable Spektor and to keep Hurley alive for physical torture). Then, in another fantastic scene, Spektor kills Stiles and is about to kill Hurley when Snap and a friend rescue the American. Snap and pal are quickly disarmed; but Nixon, not a trained murderer and revulsed at what he has seen between Spektor and Stiles, kills Spektor in a spectacular gunfight in total darkness, only to receive a fatal wound himself before Spektor falls. Nixon dies, but Snap and Margaret are married, old man Wimble makes a killing in the market itself, and Hurley is richer than ever.

On the surface, the novel seems merely a cleverly conceived English version of an American gangster movie of the 1930's; and, perhaps, due to a lack of technical precision, that is all it really is. There is, however, within the novel a structure which suggests that it is more. Despite the fact that we identify with no character (save perhaps Snap who is likeable in a sort of substanceless, ingenuous way) and despite the fact that he is *supposed* (probably) to identify with Nixon (but cannot because Nixon is too hazily drawn), we realize that this novel embodies peculiar intrapersonal relationships which must be accounted for.

For instance, there is Hurley's association with the respected Wimble family. Hurley is a bootlegger; but more than this he is one who disregards the law totally and will be, if given the chance, a murderer. Still more incredible, he willfully allows the innocent janitor to be shot down in his place. Old man Wimble, seemingly staid, likes Hurley for the simple fact that he *is* a lawbreaker—Wimble sees at least a momentary escape from his overluxurious, uneventful existence. He tacitly condones any move Hurley makes, including getting him into a bloody gun battle, which notification of the police could have prevented. Moreover, Margaret and Snap, certainly "moral" individuals by modern society's standards, have no compunctions about dealing with a bootlegger in order to obtain the money their future happiness demands. One of the most unreal things in this book, in fact, is watching the haphazard Snap gunfight as if it has been his lifelong occupation. In return for Hurley's money, Snap provides protection. Circumstances, in short, have forced these lovers into underhanded conduct in order to escape their present less-than-happy situation.

The situation is the same for Spektor and Mary. Not that these two individuals should be considered on the same ethical plane with Snap and Margaret, but they are led to swindle and even to murder in order to escape the hold Stiles has upon them. Granted that Spektor's use of Stiles, as well as Stiles's use of Spektor, is of a much different nature than Snap's use of Hurley and Hurley's use of Snap—both are imposed situations of ethical compromise. Diagrammatically, a comparison of the two situations looks like this:

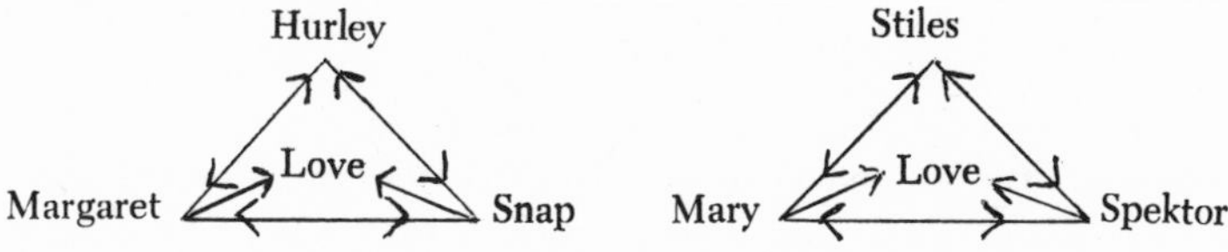

But the book contains three triangles, rather than just two. Nixon, if better presented, could have saved the novel. Nixon (at the time called Nycher) is perfectly happy with his position at the university until his landlady initiates the situation of mutual protection which blackmail involves. Once again, in order to have what is rightfully his—in Nixon's case mere contentment—he is forced to make an ethical compromise and to use for his own benefit another person equally involved in using him. He must deprive the landlady of her life; therefore, the third triangle evolves:

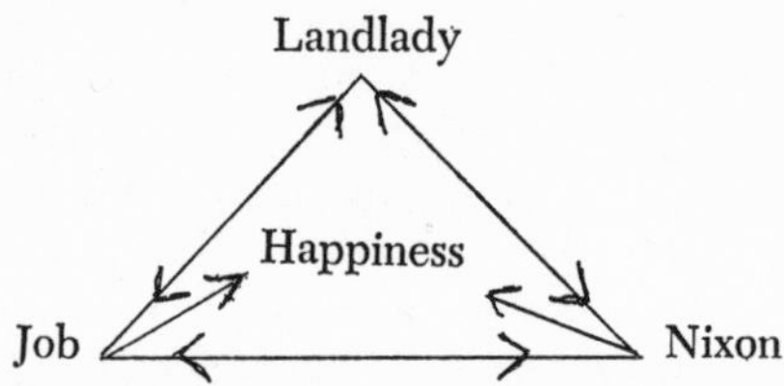

Thus, the novel's entire structure may be stated this way: (1) *The Greedy*: Hurley, Stiles, and the Landlady, in their quest for what is not rightfully theirs ensnare innocent victims; (2) *The Ensnared*: Snap, Spektor, and Nixon, no longer able to attain what is rightfully theirs by totally ethical means, enter into "mutual protection" agreements with the Greedy; (3) *The Objects*: Margaret, Mary, and Nixon's job become absolute ends; and anything done to attain them is, subjectively, right and good.

The ultimate question becomes, therefore, how many of the "Ensnared" realize that they have compromised their standards in order to outwit Fate? And the answer is that only Nixon does. Spektor, of course, is too villainous to worry about, but Nixon has (or could have) formed an effective contrast with Snap. Having shot his landlady in cold blood to promote his own comfort, Nixon, when asked by Spektor to kill Hurley, is unable to kill again. Instead, in one final effort to recoup some of his integrity, he defends Hurley from Spektor, and he and Spektor eventually kill each other. As Nixon dies he is saying to himself softly: "'One makes mistakes, I suppose,' and added in a small voice: 'Whatever that may mean.' He looked through the doorway with puzzled but contented eyes. He saw straight through Charles and the wall behind him. He left the house, passing the car, the road, the dishes and the landlady. He slipped at last through everything, leaving the body behind him to slip with gentle dignity to the ground" (275).[7]

The key phrase, I think, is "puzzled but contented eyes." The word "contented" obviously applies to the fact that he has proved himself capable of one moral action to counteract his earlier "mistake." But the puzzlement is the theme of the book, and it is better expressed in another statement about Nixon a few pages before the one just quoted: "Good guys and bad guys, it all meant nothing to Nixon. What was good and bad? It was a matter of definition. It was a ridiculous question intellectually, one that was chattered about by undergraduates. Theories, words, chatter, meaning. Anything meant anything, so long as you made it do so—or nothing in words. Stiles was a bad guy, and Wimble was a good guy. It meant nothing" (252). Snap, a "good guy," is, on the other hand, capable of no such understanding—he and Margaret are innocently but enthusiastically spending money wildly at the novel's conclusion.

In *Mrs. Dalloway*, Virginia Woolf demonstrates the fine line between sanity and insanity. In *Nostromo*, Joseph Conrad proves that honor and dishonor lurk close together in every man. In a lesser novel than either of these, White and Scott demonstrate the frightening proximity of idealism and base pragmatism. The novel fails because the authors do not subject Nixon to any kind of psychological examination until the final crescendo. Nixon, the novel's most thematically important character, is barely on stage twenty percent of the time. The novel's closing line, which is potentially tremendously effective but in the final analysis almost lost, states what the reader was prevented from realizing all along. Hurley says of Nixon: "'I was thinking of him.' . . . 'He was a good guy!'" (284).

IV Darkness at Pemberley

Darkness at Pemberley, which was written at relatively the same time as *Dead Mr. Nixon*, was published a year later. The two books are much too close in plot and structure to ensure their separate individualities, and White is not even so insistent in this book about theme as he was in his previous thriller. Readers of Jane Austen will recall Pemberley as the estate of Fitzwilliam Darcy and his wife Elizabeth Bennet; the owners of the mansion in this book are their descendants, Charles and Elizabeth Darcy. The presence of such allusions in this book, however, seems to serve no immediate purpose; but a few details, such as those noted in the chase after the kidnapped girl, do coincide.

The books are obviously the product of the same mind in the same era. Both of White's first two novels open with dual murders, in this case those of a history don named Mr. Beedon (thought to be modeled upon White's friend Potts) and a student named Mr. Fraser. Both novels depend upon the fact that the crimes are not susceptible to the usual solutions by the police, and thus the private citizens involved must defend themselves. During the defense, these people reveal themselves, though only briefly, to be capable of nearly as much evil as the criminals themselves. In each book, the hunted retreat to an old mansion and therein fortify themselves to await the onslaught of their adversary. The plot of each book is contrived, and the characterization in each is slim.

In *Darkness at Pemberley,* the forces of good are headed by Inspector Buller, who refuses to accept the Scotland Yard findings on the first two murders in Cambridge (murder and suicide over narcotics); he persists and discovers that a lecturer in chemistry named Mr. Mauleverer (who, as his name implies, represents metaphysical evil in this novel) had murdered the don in order to be next in line for the deanship of the college and had killed Fraser because he had happened to witness the crime through a window. When Buller confronts him with his theory, Mauleverer readily admits to both crimes, explains in meticulous detail how each was committed, indicates how alibis were ensured beforehand, points out to Buller that any attempt to pin the crimes on himself will result only in a libel case against the inspector, and then hints of the murder of still a third person, a drunken janitor who had seen him emerge from Fraser's apartment. This scene Sylvia Warner calls "an early example of White's talent for irrefutability."[8] Mauleverer triumphs temporarily and Buller is hamstrung; in his disillusionment and horror, he quits the police force. This action ends the first part of the novel.

The conversion to the second part is ridden by a structural disunity which is never overcome. Buller has gone to Pemberley with the Darcys, his friends of long-standing, in Derbyshire to escape his failure. Several things go artistically wrong here. The handful of characters (all except Buller and Mauleverer) in whom the reader had become interested is dropped entirely, and a new, heretofore-unseen group appears—Charles and Elizabeth Darcy (sister and brother) and the congenial parasites and local servants who inhabit their large estate. Obviously White wanted Buller, the lone inspector, out of his previous role and into a human situation; but the transferal is unbelievable—and especially so is the way he transfers Mauleverer himself into the new group. The villain was willing to let Buller fester; and, since Buller has no evidence, there is no reason why Mauleverer should pursue him. Thus, the author must construct an elaborate and otherwise irrelevant association in the mind of Charles Darcy to accomplish the necessary juncture. Charles, who has spent two years in prison for transporting narcotics for another man (these were discovered in his car after an accident in which his own wife lost her life) decides to murder Mauleverer, of whom he has heard Buller speak, as a retaliation against the addict on whose account his wife was killed. In the dark of night, he travels to Cambridge, threatens Mauleverer to his face, thinks better of it, and returns home. Buller is furious that his adversary has been stirred up; and Mauleverer soon secrets himself in Pemberley to gain revenge. The next day, while Charles is walking in the stable, a tile falls from the ceiling and narrowly misses his head. Charles thinks this an accident, but Buller knows better.

Amidst this and much more obvious contrivance, the reader is hard pressed to catch the philosophical question which White and his characters put forth and only occasionally think about: if society is unable to prove the guilt of one of its members of a horrendous and bloodthirsty crime (or three of them), does an individual or group who is sure of the criminal's guilt have the ethical duty to ensure his punishment? By the end of the book, the question seems to have been forgotten; but the answer may be an implicit yes—as long as the action is taken for the protection of society and not for satisfaction of the personal hatred of the avenging individual or group.

White rejects the plot of the stereotyped thriller in that he refuses to allow any apparent friend to be in league with Mauleverer in order, first, to produce a more logical explanation for the fact that the man moves so easily about the house and, second, to yield a more startling ending to the story itself. Mauleverer, though always as much out of the reader's view as he is out of that of the characters, acts alone—a fact that is never in doubt. What metaphysical implications the story possesses (many, though all are only slightly drawn) are heightened by this solitariness and unaided fluidity of the evil principle.

Hate and fear, of course, naturally motivate the group in Charles's house to rid the place of its hidden adversary. When a search of the grounds proves futile and when a series of startling terror devices are dropped upon them by their omnipresent enemy, Buller calls in a former police crony for help. Charles is kept under constant guard, and no one eats anything which has not been newly taken from a sealed tin. After several more incidents of nighttime terror, it is determined that Mauleverer is lurking in the elaborate chimney system of the house. When Buller decides that poison gas should be pumped through the entire system, Elizabeth Darcy (whom Buller secretly loves, and she loves him in Jane Austen fashion) reprimands him for hatred, inhumanity, and cowardice in the face of the unknown. Buller, ashamed of himself, requests that only something on the order of tear gas be employed. On the night before the gas arrives, however, all the men in the house take positions by all water faucets since they are certain that Mauleverer must occasionally come from the chimneys for a drink. In a semicomical scene (of which there are several in the book), Mauleverer, dressed in black, drops beside each guard without being seen; and, in retaliation for their selfishness, he murders an old servant. Hatred of Mauleverer wells up in the household (Elizabeth included); and on the next day, poison gas is pumped into the chimneys. Following this event the house sleeps quietly, having assumed that Mauleverer is dead.

Throughout the book, White unobtrusively emphasizes the dichotomy between appearances and reality in Mauleverer's (evil's) behavior. This same night, Elizabeth is taken from her bed by a figure in black. A short time later Buller is notified by a chauffeur that one of the estate's cars has been removed from the garage. Finding Elizabeth missing, Buller and his friends set out on a chase in three different cars. They follow Mauleverer's well-distributed clues until, on a deserted road, they run over a pile of nails which Mauleverer has distributed also. As they fix their tires, Mauleverer returns to Pemberley to kill Charles. That night, when all have returned in despair,

Buller decides to look in on his friend before retiring. As he opens the door, he sees Mauleverer about to commit the crime. This scene is followed by a long chase through the chimneys, the discovery of Elizabeth's paralyzed body in one of them, Buller's own capture by the evil man, and a long speech by Mauleverer (in the chimney) in which he tells the helpless Buller that he is truly sorry to have to destroy him, but his evil vanity demands an outlet for its cleverness which society obviously does not provide. He chides Buller for not realizing that people who live in chimneys usually carry gas masks with them, thus explaining his escape from the poison. While Mauleverer is dragging Elizabeth to her death, Buller breaks loose, catches up with the murderer on the roof, and wrestles him over the side.

Once again, this is a story of a cleverly contrived plot with two-dimensional characters and, unfortunately, two-dimensional evil. One of the most noticeable flaws in White's later books is his inability to limit the number of subjects he chooses to discuss in any one book, even in the finest volume of the Arthurian tetralogy, *The Ill-Made Knight.* Thus, many things introduced are only partially developed. Here, in a book which attempts to develop far fewer ideas (really only the nature of evil, though this admittedly is an infinite subject), White demonstrates a similar inability to discuss things at the right time or ever to discuss them thoroughly. White seems to be over-interested in the ramifications of his plot *qua* plot, and thus the characters often respond to the philosophical and ethical questions involved in the same blind manner in which they respond to the false leads with which Mauleverer provides them. In short, it is one thing not to understand evil, but it is quite another to forget to ask the pertinent questions. Though White does not intend to, I am sure, he makes his characters seem quite absentminded about greater issues.

This novel is the end of the detective story *per se* for White, though several future books indicate his innate love for the genre. *Mistress Masham's Repose* and *The Master* are obvious examples. In his next two books, the Aston novels, White concentrates purely on character development and interaction; and, as a result, he produces two dull books. In the volume following the Aston books, however—*Farewell Victoria*—he achieves a small masterpiece.

V They Winter Abroad

One thing White was never meant to be as an author was an entertainer of intellectuals who cared only to be intellectually entertained, and the two "Aston" novels are ample evidence of this fact. *They Winter Abroad* (1932), while better than *First Lesson* (1932), is the product of a young novelist still seeking both a style and a milieu. Whereas White's forte is the creation of larger-than-life characters doing unbelievable things, he attempts in these two novels to have average people doing average things. But White is no Aldous Huxley, and the result is average at best. *They Winter Abroad* received a sour review from David Garnett in the *New Statesman and Nation*, but the review itself opened the way for the great friendship between the two men which was to begin four years later in 1936.

White often referred to this novel as his "Huxley novel," that is, a story which revolves around one cynically handled topic of discussion instead of the traditional development of plot. There is almost no plot in this book, and whatever substance it contains derives from the interaction of several (too many) characters as they pour forth (or keep in) their ideas on the subject of *love*. All the characters, with one exception, are Englishmen vacationing for the winter in Positano, Italy. Most are present because it is "the thing to do"; some are there because they have nothing else to do. The story is split into two distinct halves: the first half is an introduction to the characters involved as well as to the individual problems and/or pettinesses of each; the second half is a demonstration of the characters formed by these problems and/or pettinesses as they function, either practically or theoretically, within the realm of love.

The novel opens on a misleading note, for White takes some pains to divide the group into the "drawing-room set" and the "smoking-room set." At first, the reader expects to see a two-team battle on the topic involved, but the novel is actually one of individual reactions to love rather than one of common denominators. True, the smoking-room set is more liberal than the drawing-room set; but, if the story is to be saved at all, the distinction is best dropped—and even White ceases to make it for long periods.

The characters, all with "type" names, represent typical positions about love. Their exchanges are mildly amusing at best, but occasionally genuine poignancy is connected with a given individual. At the center of the entire morass, standing technically alone but somehow connected with the responses of all the others, is an intellectual bore known only as "The Professor." Ensnarled in theory, the professor constantly espouses a rather self-oriented variation of platonic love—specifically, a love which allows freedom of escape at all times. The Professor constantly chides those indulging in more committal forms, and he repeatedly warns those not yet committed but inclining toward each other. The novel which then becomes a series of definitions of "love," lists the etymologies and enumerates the connotations in each definition. To one side of the professor are those who, for one reason or another, are not involved (though they would like to be) and to the other are those who, in one way or another, are involved (whether they want to be or not).

The abstainers include, first of all, the elderly Mrs. Skimlit, an affected Irish Protestant who claims never to have been in love and who defensively shuns the lack of attention she receives from most of the other guests at the Santo Biagio. More sympathetic is Miss Albino, a fortyish, lonely spinster who had received a proposal of marriage twenty years before and had declined it in order to experience pursuit by a male—but she was not pursued. In unconscious retaliation, she became both the clerk at the Santo Biagio (to live in the area where her happiness almost materialized) and the head of the local animal-protection societies (to foist upon dumb creatures what she failed to foist upon intelligent ones). Like Mrs. Skimlit, she stoically faces a negative future. With this pair are two obese sisters, the Misses Cowfold, who are too homely and too shy to depart their mutual protection, but who are miserable all the time they endure each other.

The most tragic of this group, however, is a middle-aged man who is significantly named Mr. McInvert. Superstitious and misanthropic, McInvert, on the present trip to Italy, finds the fear of death and a chaotic afterlife forcing him into human relationships he has hitherto shunned. The Professor works furiously to keep him uncommitted—and succeeds. At the conclusion of the novel, however, McInvert tells him that his semiplatonic relationships are totally unnatural; and he despairs as he does so about the waste of his life. Suddenly attacked by one of the young ladies of the group, a Miss Prune who is a member of the opposite group, McInvert rejects her invitation to bed and hurls himself off a cliff. He is afraid, since he has terminal tuberculosis, to establish the human relationship that the Professor has repeatedly told him to be futile and selfish.

If life in aquiescent harmony with the Professor's ideas brings loneliness and nihilism, life in enthusiastic rejection of them brings little better. The young college graduate, Mr. Pupillary (whom White curiously calls the hero of the novel, even though several other characters have larger roles), has come to Italy for "kicks" only to find himself falling in love with a peasant girl ironically and Chaucerianly called Costanza.[9] Whereas Chaucer's Custance sailed faithfully all over the inhabited world, Pupillary's is married when he returns from a one-day boat trip to Capri. Pupillary, formerly love-them-and-leave-them himself, has, after finally committing himself to the lifelong love of one person (he objects fiercely to the Professor's inference that it will be otherwise), been loved and left.

While Pupillary pursues Costanza, young Anne Menzies (engaged and disengaged two years before) hotly pursues Pupillary. Feeling an indefinable poetic attraction to the young man, Anne never discovers that he has no feeling for her. The hitherto coarse young man is, at the end of the novel, trying to determine how to free himself of her without breaking her all-too-certain heart. The chain of Anne-Pupillary-Costanza verifies, theoretically at least, many of the Professor's arguments concerning the inherent heartbreak lurking in every love relationship which is a love of anything more than the mind.

Similar to Anne Menzies, thought not so fortunate, is the buck-toothed Miss Prune, heretofore unnoticed by men and too "illogically moral" to generate interest in herself. Now, finding the respectable Dr. Arnold-Browne attracted to her, the briefly incautious Miss Prune finds herself suddenly seduced. Initially horrified by her own liberality, Miss Prune changes her mind and unsuccessfully propositions the confused Mr. McInvert. At the end of the novel, Miss Prune is confused and disoriented.

Dr. Arnold-Browne, himself, is not a run-of-the-mill rapist. He has had a lifelong, uncontrollable attraction to young and innocent girls, despite the fact he is, on the surface, happily married. Periodically, he convinces himself that he should seduce such a girl, yet contemporaneously he is confronted by hazy notions of morality and God. During his present seduction, the Holy Ghost and Miss Prune collide in the action. Having seduced her, the notion of God fades from the doctor's mind in favor of the more terrifying concept of public scandal.

And so, in the final analysis, the Professor is a bore and too much the antithesis of a "dirty old man," but he seems to be right. The have-not's may be lonely, but the momentary-have's are totally frustrated and disillusioned. The reader and White grope for an alternative, but the only people who present themselves are the married couples—the Australian Joneses, the parents of Anne Menzies; and perhaps the pre-Prune Arnold-Brownes. They are all married, they seldom argue, but they are bored with each other, despite personal assurances that they are totally happy. So marriage cannot be the ideal either. Perhaps the most positive remark that can be made about the situation White presents in his "Huxley novel" is that those who have loved and committed themselves seem more satisfactory as humans than those who receded from involvement.

The novel itself contains very little physical action (beyond conversation). Even when the characters take sightseeing trips, the group manages to discuss the usual topic. However, two scenes are particularly well drawn. The first occurs in Chapter 13 where Mrs. Skimlit, the Menzies, and others are in church "loving God" while the absent members are out on the beach or the cliffs loving each other. While Mrs. Arnold-Browne listlessly gazes out the church window, Dr. Arnold-Browne enthusiastically seduces Miss Prune. While Anne Menzies thinks more about John Pupillary than about Jesus Christ, John Pupillary is experimenting to see how far toward Costanza's panties he can maneuver his hand before she stops him. The constant scene shifting between the church and the little orgies forms an effective statement about the impossibility of real love in any form. The second outstanding scene comes in Chapter 15, where, after a full day of debate about, and the practice of, love (all definitions), each of the main characters is shown going to bed (or staying up as the case may be). Miss Albino cries herself to sleep, dreaming of her dead Pekingnese. Mrs. Skimlit is secure in "her room" away from those who usually and ungraciously fail to succumb to her will. Mr. Pupillary cannot go to sleep for want of Costanza, and Anne Menzies cannot go to bed for want of Mr. Pupillary. Mr. McInvert furiously writes the story of his life, a story which in substance is "a protest against authority, a vehement position of right" (239). Only the Menzies and the Joneses sleep peacefully, for only they are snoring rather than dreaming about impossible love.

Perhaps one of the most noticeable lacks in the early White novels, especially the very bland "Aston" books, is the absence of the short satiric jabs White's later novels consistently throw. Not that the attempt is not made in the Aston novels—rather, they seem to strike too softly and to be slightly off target. One of the few that comes close to real satiric wit in *They Winter Abroad* is this statement about the "equality" of British women:

> But the Englishwoman, thought Mr. Pupillary, is different. She is her husband's equal, yes, but she must be given seats by tired and returning city workers; she must not be required to walk too far or carry her own handbag; she must be supplied with cigarettes and free dinners by persons who stand whilst addressing her and run for her ashtrays; she must be catered for by a special vocabulary which omits certain words and stories on the principle that nobody has ever heard of them; the hat must be doffed on encountering her. (59–60)[10]

Even this passage does not meet the standard of the tetralogy or the Irish books; and, for a novel whose format depends upon such humor and such incisive comment, the lack of it is terribly evident. *First Lesson* is even less strong.

VI First Lesson

Even after expurgation, *First Lesson* is one of White's "raciest" books, and he was forced to maintain the pseudonym he had established for his previous book—James Aston. The parents of Stowe students would not, obviously, take kindly to a novel about a don who, at the age of forty-seven, had decided to dispense with his morals. However, since Chatto and Windus sent all the correspondence about the book to James Aston at Stowe, the mail distribution routed it all to a student, one James Ashton, who disclosed that White was the actual author. Because of this incident and because Chatto had made some cuts in the book to remove some of its more daring passages, White negotiated an American contract by himself, leaving his English publisher in the lurch when he had found an American publisher. For several reasons, then, this book was White's last to be published by Chatto and Windus.

First Lesson is, in most ways, a poor book. The characters are better than some of those in his early novels such as *Dead Mr. Nixon*; but they are not nearly lively enough to keep the book floating through its allegorical plotlessness. Although humorous in several places, the story is not one in which humor can be a sufficient distraction.

The novel is about a middle-aged university don who is off on sabbatical to Naples with the intention, for reasons never made entirely clear, of losing his long-kept virginity. When Joseph Belfry is bored in Naples, he sails for Capri, an island where he falls in with a heterogeneous, loose crowd. Despite the efforts of one girl named Eulalia to relieve him of his chastity, Belfry is determined to lose it only to a beautiful waitress named Beatrice. Beatrice, isolated and misused on tiny Capri, sees in Belfry an opportunity for escape, luxury, and pink underwear about which she constantly dreams. When Belfry, after losing his virginity in the clumsiest of ways possible, offers to row her back to the mainland on the condition that she live with him (but not go to bed with him until she is ready), she tacitly decides never to go to bed with him but vocally agrees to sail and live according to the contract. Having taken up residence in Anfitrano, they quickly fall in with an even odder bunch of characters who offer Beatrice (and Belfry if he can sustain it) the life she has never known. Do what he may, Belfry is unable to penetrate the makeshift wall which divides their room in half nor even maintain her attention in public. Beatrice is attracted to a traveling salesman on the beach, and it is many months before he leaves town. Until this attraction occurs, Belfry has been allowed only two hours each morning with his intended mistress while she teaches him Italian; after the salesman appears, Belfry tosses all pride aside and begs to be allowed in her bed. Feeling that Belfry and his money will vanish if she doesn't agree, Beatrice allows Belfry in her bed on Tuesdays and Saturdays. This situation debases both; as a result, Belfry pleads with her to love him, and Beatrice demands more freedom from the man she considers too old and too unsatisfactory as a lover. After numerous attempts by Belfry to prevent Beatrice's leaving, she elopes with a Russian named Platonov, leaving poor Belfry to return to England and the stale existence he had, for a year, escaped.

The novel is full of Beatrice, readings in Dante and quotations from him, and characters who often resemble certain Dantesque phenomena; therefore, some allegorical equations are seemingly intended. Since the allegory is at best confused and at worst insubstantial and unprofitable, we will concentrate here only upon the general outlines. Dante, at the opening of the "Inferno" calls himself a middle-aged man who midway in life found himself lost in a dark wood; and the way out is not evident. Belfry, after forty-seven years of life and twenty-five of teaching school, feels generally the same, since, just as Dante felt his Catholicism to be impotent, his scholarly devotion to the dictates of the Age of Reason had never been put into practice. He seeks "the purified ecstacy [*sic*] of a second birth"(7)[11] in order to enter, as Dante did, a new life. The rest of the comparison between Belfry and Dante is, of course, ironic. Unwilling to fight through the Inferno and the Purgatorio before attaining happiness, Belfry lunges right into the Paradiso and quickly locates his Beatrice.

Beatrice's history has its ironies: "She had been seduced in Bologna, by a merchant who had come north to buy wine which would eventually be sold as Lacrima Christi; and he had persuaded her to fly with him to Naples. Within a few months they had been quarreling bitterly, for Beatrice was a cut above the docile masochism of the south, and the girl had found herself abandoned with the equivalent of five English pounds" (7–8).

Out on her own, she works as a waitress in an establishment which demands overtime as a prostitute. Prostitution she virtuously avoids, as Beatrice would, but again in an ironic sort of way: "Though she had evaded prostitution, she had no objections to a lover; except those of caution. If he were very rich and beautiful, she would accept him with delight; even with a medium share of these commodities she would have been content" (10). Very quickly Dante-Belfry meets his Beatrice, and the ludicrous search for the "right way" begins.

If Dante's Beatrice represents the spiritual force of revelation, Belfry's is a purely physical force who is useless until her physique is revealed. If Dante's Beatrice is an active leader, Belfry's is no better than a passive one—for, if Belfry learns anything from her (and he certainly does—his *first* real *lesson,* in fact), he does so by tracing her whereabouts each time she heartlessly abandons him for more attractive men.

The symbolic encounters of the book's central chapters are very obscure—the fact that they are lifeless and unproductive in the long run seems to be the most important common denominator of all of them. Perhaps the most ironic employment of the analogy with Dante is the fact that Beatrice *does* lead Belfry to the truth. Her constant rejection of him and her selfishness toward him force him to realize that he is attempting to buy his happiness on earth by purchasing the worldly. She teaches him the difference between love and lust, a distinction that he in his previous nonsensual life has never made. Perhaps the book's most telling exchange comes on the day she finally leaves him forever. Belfry tells her, as he has page after page in this extremely repetitive novel, that she should marry him and return with him to Cambridge: " 'Perhaps you wouldn't be unhappy. It would be an assured income. . .' " (262). She replies, teaching him the first lesson of life that she herself has only recently learned: " 'I love Platonov.' " By confessing to both herself and him that she *loves* the rancorous Russian, she has simultaneously revealed what has been wrong with their relationship from the first—he thought he could buy happiness; she thought happiness came from being bought.

Though Beatrice teaches Belfry certain truths about himself and about life, she does not, as Dante's heroine does, lead to anything faintly resembling the beatific vision. For example, we may contrast the final paragraph of each work. First Dante's: "To the high fantasy her power failed; but now my desire and my will were revolved, like a wheel which was moved evenly, by the Love which moves the sun and other stars."[12] And in White's, Belfry is watching three cigarettes disintegrating as they revolve around a toilet bowl: "So he fetched a fork from the gyp-room (disturbing Mrs. Sniggs, who was reading a periodical called *The Boys' Magazine*) and the waste-paper basket from the study. He knelt down in front of the bowl and began delving with the fork. The yellow strands became quite unravelled and floated to the edges of the basin" (267). The circular motions described at the end of each work have other differences, obviously, than being merely centripetal and centrifugal, respectively.

While it is still difficult to recognize the White capable of the Arthurian tetralogy, *Mistress Masham's Repose*, and *The Goshawk*, his characterization at least shows some signs of strengthening in *First Lesson*. Had he created characters equal to these in *Dead Mr. Nixon* he might have produced stronger early novels than he did. Belfry is just colorless enough to be believable as the prude-turned-lecher he attempts to be. His efforts to reverse his entire life are initially comic but are eventually tragic in a gray, unviolent manner. The tension between his natural reserve and his forced libido is always nicely balanced. Belfry is an undynamic man who impresses us as a pathetically passive character.

Beatrice is also successful, though I must initially agree with the young reader quoted by Sylvia Warner[13] who remarked that she seemed more like a boy. She never intrigues the reader as the voluptuous, enticing beauty that all the central characters feel she is, but she does serve as an effective blotter for all of Belfry's good (and evil) intentions. Having been hurt once, she now feels the world owes her something—and Belfry serves as the world's agent. She is every moment selfish and unsympathetic with her benefactor, but hers is actually the only behavior which could make him realize the folly of his middle age.

The lesser characters are at least momentarily memorable. Platonov, the vain Russian who prides himself (and his mistress) on the fact that he can handle two women at once; Signorina Ugly, who dances and twirls on tables and wears no underwear; Don Vincenzo, the mad psychologist who imports an equally mad girlfriend and dyes his beard to please her; Roon, the painter, who takes pity on Belfry and tries to teach him how to force Beatrice into submission—these are original and entertaining creations. Their stagnation in a stale, repetitive, tritely symbolic plot, however, makes them exist as unrelated individual entities, almost types, rather than as crucial parts of a dynamic whole.

Perhaps, in retrospect, the quality White later developed which these early novels lack is resonance—the ability to sound many related themes within a fictional situation. Early in his career, White builds all parts toward one rather cut and dried, often hackneyed, piece of moralism—in *First Lesson,* it is the conquest of true love over lust; in *Dead Mr. Nixon,* it was the corruptibility of even the most incorruptible human spirits—a theme which Joseph Conrad, Herman Melville, and William Faulkner excel in to such an extent as to make White's attempt little more than a dull thud. Not until White's next novel, *Farewell Victoria,* is he finally able to combine the witty style, the noble simplicity of plot and character, the resonant themes, and his natural compassion for all things forced to endure life on earth into a successful work which is, if not representative of his absolute best, clearly indicative of it.

CHAPTER 3

The Years Before Arthur

I Farewell Victoria

FAREWELL VICTORIA was written in what Sylvia Warner terms the helter-skelter period of the early 1930's; it was the best book to come out of that group and one of the books upon which White's fame today depends. It did not sell well when first released; but it has since been reissued in both England and America, and an entirely new illustrated edition has recently appeared in Britain. It is one of the few early volumes for which White enlisted no outside help.

After six books of questionable merit and success, White demonstrates a substantial talent in *Farewell Victoria.* The novel is intended to represent three-quarters of a century of British history as it is reflected in one human being. Written in seven parts, each shows the hero, a horsegroom known only as Mundy (*Mundi,* world?), in one crucial and formative moment in his life. Part I displays him in 1858, when he is only eight years old; and it is meant to be representative of both his childhood and of England in the mid-nineteenth century. Part II concerns the year 1875; Mundy, now twenty-five, is a forlorn, deserted husband who is trying to survive what seems like an eternally broken heart. Part III takes place in 1899, when Mundy is in the Boer War; and he faces for the first time in his guarded life the mass destruction that man has learned to wreak upon his fellows. Part IV occurs in 1901, the year in which Queen Victoria dies and in which the lonely soldier returns from Zululand and takes his second wife. Part V, 1918, is a year of the battles of World War I, and the year in which Mundy's only son (by his first wife) is killed on the battlefields of France. In Part VI, 1929, Mundy, now seventy-nine, returns from his profitless job to find his second wife dead in her chair; and

Part VII shows Mundy on his death bed in 1933. No section attempts to picture more than one day's activities in a given year—thus White has attempted to tell the story of Mundy and England merely by relating seven days in seventy-five years; and he succeeds fabulously well.

Farewell Victoria is a masterpiece, minor only because of its relatively short length. For the first time White has a book full of human beings rather than stilted, ego-coached, pseudo-intellectuals who resemble human beings no more than fish do. Their human qualities, especially Mundy's, never suffer, despite the author's desire to have Mundy symbolize England itself. There are no types, even though the situation is one that could typecast characters very easily. And neither is the story—despite what the overbrief outline presented above may make it seem—tragic, hopeless, existentially absurd, or any of the things that stereotyped novels, written along the same lines as this one, so often are. The admirable qualities in Mundy, and in the human race for that matter, are that they cling tenaciously to humanism and inspire it in others despite the mechanization and destruction with which the world conspires to counter them. Life in *Farewell Victoria* is not brief and futile; it is long and rewarding, and the difficulties that confront one who truly lives life are exactly the things which make the sheer length of it productive of meaningful repayments. A statement White makes about Mundy late in the novel summarizes this poignantly. Mundy, alone and very old, stands on the seashore musing: "Life was like that, when one thought about its length or brevity. The poets called it short because they had their eyes upon eternity. They resented the brief and bursting joys, wanted a million more of them" (229).[1]

Such an understanding of Mundy's life does not mean that, by way of allegory, England is found to be faultless in the novel. Actually the book, with a main character who embodies such a positive attitude, is actually a picture of man castrating what seems to be a ravaging Fate. White clearly presents the life and activities of 1858 in a more glorious light than those of any later year. Victoria seems throughout the book to be a symbol of what England once was and never will be again. More than this, she is a symbol of individual humanity; for during her reign men led free and unencumbered lives. Not that this life was always blissful, Mundy's wife's desertion is evidence of that; but it is certainly more acceptable than the situations that were to come later. As Victoria dies, men are killed in a senseless war in an obscure African country; industrialization begins to regiment man's body and trample his spirit after the turn of the century; and King Edward assists by polluting the air with his newfangled motor car. Yet the man whose true humanism lifts him above what humanity *en masse* causes is truly heroic in an anti-Prufrockian sense. And this man White glorifies through the character of Mundy in *Farewell Victoria.*

Part I (1858) presents young eight-year-old Mundy at his first home on the estate of Ambleden, a place referred to constantly in this novel as a symbol of freedom and tranquility, not ideally but comparatively so. (It would be well to emphasize here, I think, that this is definitely a Realistic and not a Utopian novel.) Mundy, the son of a groom, spends even his holidays contentedly learning his father's trade. Around him is the family of Sir William, the landowner; and happiness is obviously not confined to those who are, as Mundy is, of servile rank. This first part contains little plot—it is, rather, a portrait of English life which is truly representative of the English spirit. The most important incident in the section occurs when a woman, known throughout Mundy's recollections only as Milady, takes the little urchin in hand and points out Lady Catherine de Bourgh, telling him "don't forget her" (24). Rather than being Mundy's incentive to rebel against those who have more than he does, as such an anonymous "noble" figure is in so many proletarian books, he remembers Lady Catherine forever as a symbol of that which makes life itself a glamorous and worthwhile undertaking. In fact, when Mundy is on his deathbed in the final chapter of the novel, his doctor persuades him to name his most memorable moment. Reflecting over a life which was at times happy, at times less so—but always meaningful—he cites this single vision of Lady Catherine as the most inspirational.

The internal sections balance fates nicely. In Part II, a part which White frames in sarcastic references to the wreck of the

Deutschland and Hopkins's poem about it, Mundy is crushed by the death of his first child (apparently illegitimately conceived), by the desertion of his wife (whom he loves but is unable to intrigue), and by the disappearance of his second child (with its mother). Unlike Hopkins, who White implies was horrified by the sea-wreck but who too easily assumed that the nuns aboard went down singing hymns (White is vehement about the fact that Hopkins was home in bed while the whole tragedy took place), Mundy pulls himself through the events which nearly destroy him in more human, less improbable ways. Despite the fact that he takes to drink now and then, Mundy manages to bury the past. Not that he does it overnight—it seems more likely that it required a decade to accomplish. The point that the author is so insistent upon is that the human spirit, which includes within itself a desire to live and to be happy while doing so, is allowed to fight its way back to health. Perhaps the most noticeable characteristic of Mundy's spiritual resurgence is his refusal to poison the remainder of his life with the hate he initially felt for the man who stole his wife. Again we have White's insistence on realism—Mundy *wants* to hate, and he is far from being above it. The positive value is in his conquest of his natural desire.

If the novel to this point seems arcadian, the war scenes in Part III negate the assumption. The pictures are realistic in the same way that Stephen Crane's Henry Fleming's or Ernest Hemingway's Frederic Henry's are. Mundy, in his supreme desire to "live and let live," takes advantage of a rout to desert the battle entirely. Throughout the section dealing with Mundy's military tour, which he first involves himself in as a means of escaping his memory-laden life in England, White intersperses the gore of the African battlefield with newspaper clippings recounting the trivialities that entertain the uninvolved in England. On the one hand, the author seems to be emphasizing the degeneration of England itself which, far now from being the place of humanism and individualism, can recline and allow great numbers of its population to die in a futile fight against an enigmatic enemy. But, on the other hand, Mundy, still fighting the failures of his past (he is in his late forties now), comes to realize the value of just being alive. More than this, he realizes the need for positive assertion in the face of a world which seemingly becomes every day more hostile. Before the tragic battle of Isandula, White reflects upon his hero this way: "Mundy had not discovered that he was living in a changing world. He was too close to the Sixties to realize their beauty; too young to see that they were dying, or at least changing to something else" (90). What he takes away from Africa is the will to preserve, at least in his private life, the beauty of the 1860's despite the ugliness forecast by the new century.

Unlike Fleming, Mundy does not return to fight, and he also does not bury himself away to await doom and dry rot. Part IV opens with the death and funeral of Queen Victoria which, symbolically, is the death of humanism and the birth of industrialization and human insignificance. Yet on the day of the funeral, Mundy, at the age of fifty-one, marries his second wife, Alice, a person of similar background to his own; Alice is representative of a personal preservation of happiness and integrity despite the existential odds-makers. Both Mundy and his new wife have been working for several years for a countess of Russian extraction. The woman is of the wrong nationality and the wrong physique (seven feet, six inches tall); thus, life is closed to her. Yet she serves as a model for Mundy in her charity and her raw will to endure despite the criticizing majority. Mundy, as her chauffeur, admires her and identifies with her.

White effectively emphasizes Mundy's heroic struggle by means of the passage of the normal course of events. All of Mundy's old friends and relatives die, yet each death inspires the aging man with a new will to live. The death (in World War I) of his son in Part V brings one of the man's most outwardly philosophical reflections. This section, though short, has Mundy placing himself first within the entire context of historical humanity and then within the context of historical and national disaster. Needing reassurance because of this most recent tragedy, he reflects upon the fact that man, the human race, has continued despite such things as the Norman Conquest, Black Death, and the like; and he resolves that it must have been the will of the species, composed of the individual wills of individual men, to survive—to stand up to life and take more. Despite his son's death, Part V ends on a note of great joy.

All the sections after Mundy's experience in the Boer War take place in or around the town of St. Leonards, the opposite of Ambleden in that it represents a time and a place where the individual must struggle for his own integrity and preservation rather than have it ready-made for him (as in Ambleden). The name Leonard means "one who is strong or brave as a lion," and such behavior, rather than natural piety, canonizes saints in the twentieth-century world.

In Part VI the note of hopefulness that concluded the previous section is continued. This part emphasizes the fact that, even though now in their late seventies, Mundy and Alice have succeeded in making a fruitful life for each other. Mundy is the town's last hackney driver (everyone else has become motorized). He continues, for curiosity's sake, to drive the countess's horse and carriage, transporting a very occasional rider from the train station to his home. By so doing Mundy preserves what he loves—the animals he was trained to groom, the memory of the countess he found so inspirational, and the memory of a past age which embodied humanity at its highest powers. The fact that he makes no monetary profit does not discourage him. One of the book's most memorable moments comes as Mundy, on a cold night, waits around the station for the last evening train, despite the fact that he yearns to return to his warm home and his beloved elderly wife. The train arrives and no one rides with him. He goes home happy nonetheless, only to find his wife dead at her knitting.

In Part VII, the climax of Mundy's own life, the scene takes place four years after Alice's death. Mundy is now back to grooming horses, a job that, even at eighty-three, he still does well. After a day's work he walks to the seashore and experiences a culmination of his love for humanity and his desire to live. In several poetically beautiful paragraphs, he is described as being at one with all men, all time, and all space. He is, in short, yearning for an eternity he cannot define and of which he is nonetheless afraid. White draws a brilliant contrast in the final pages of the book, as Mundy lies on his death bed. First he speaks of man and his country:

> The old man on the bed had been born in the country, but in a country where people had existed by themselves. They still tried to do so. And for that reason, because they were individuals as they had always been, they were enemies of the modern state. They had never been from home before, but now they were being evicted. Villages, which had not known more than three peasants out of work, were now able to boast of sixty. . . . They would make no protests about their characters, no complaints about their fortune, no attempts to increase charity. (250)

And then White speaks of this man, Mundy, here obviously symbolic of the raw human spirit and the will to survive and even, if possible to rule: "The old man's story had been more fully historical than that of Queen Victoria, because it had been one of simple life. He had run parallel to Europe, making the picture human. Life . . . had been the dependent of great events, but the great events had not been principally important to it" (251).

Yet this theme still has one more ramification, and even this fact the hero realized vividly during the second half of his life. He had been miserable during the first half of his life—miserable in the very Victorian age which was supposedly so conducive to, and so representative of, human freedom, individuality, and happiness. Yet in the second half, the age of impersonality and destruction, an age antithetical to the individual man, he was happier than he had ever been before. While this is obviously not a last-minute condemnation on White's part of all he has praised, it is probably a statement of the fact that, inherent in his nature, man has a desire to demonstrate and defend the freedom which is so individually his own. Unchallenged, freedom and individuality are impotent; threatened, however, they prove themselves either tremendously frail or, as in Mundy's case, valiantly heroic. *Farewell Victoria,* a novel of the potentiality of human beings even in a universe bordering constantly on nihilism, is one of White's finest and most beautiful achievements.

II Earth Stopped

Despite the fact that he seemed to find himself in *Farewell Victoria* and despite the fact that his next two novels received some favorable reviews at the time of their publication (even some enthusiastic ones), White's two "Stowe" novels seem to me representative of his poorest work. *The Observer* reviewed *Earth Stopped* (1934) as a book that would make the reader laugh until he ached; the *Sunday Times* called it a "diverting frolic" and a "feast of good things"; the *Daily Mail* found it "incessantly amusing." Even Graham Greene, writing in *The Spectator,* was laudatory: "Very, Very funny. . . . Mr. White's descriptions of hunting are often as aesthetically exciting as those of Mr. Sassoon's 'Foxhunting Man.' "[2] Sylvia Warner, however, who seems to feel as I do, calls the book "haggard with intellect" and full of "jokes which fail to amuse."[3]

There are several tenuous reasons for the divergence of opinion. The first could be the fact that the contemporary reviewers were examining the book as a curious entity in itself, as entertaining reading for a certain class at a certain time in a certain place. The modern reader, however, tends—if he knows anything at all of White's later, much better work—to begin comparing it unfavorably with these more representative products. Secondly, the fox-hunting syndrome which so possessed the Stowe crowd is obviously less real, for different reasons, to Miss Warner and myself (and to *most* American readers, I am afraid). A third reason for the seeming failure of the book, one somewhat connected with the second, is that White satirizes fox-hunting and its participants so much better elsewhere—in works both earlier and later than *Earth Stopped.*[4] The present novel, with the exception of one or two scenes, is pale by contrast.

However, fox-hunting is not the sole subject of this book. Rather, it is a conglomeration of philosophy, political comment, love affairs, slapstick comedy, and various degrees and brands of sadism. Perhaps the main flaw, in retrospect, is the fact that this multitude of purposes is entrusted to characters who are essentially substanceless and too many in number. White seems to be regressing to sins so prominent several years before in his fiction.

The axis of the plot of *Earth Stopped* is the Woodmansterne estate of the Tenth Earl of Scamperdale at which he has collected a rather anomalous assortment of parasites who seem to be around for nothing more than pursuing foxes, fishes, and each other, and languishing in their own wealthless rank at the Earl's expense. Most of the characters involved are interesting only when the status and ennui they so treasure are challenged by fate, Communists, or, in the end, open warfare. The one exception among them is a young English Communist who has appropriately changed his name to John Marx. At first Marx is cynically critical of all he sees at Woodmansterne, and the reader wonders, as does the establishment of the estate, why he remains there. The truth is soon evident to the reader (although not to the other characters) that Marx, at a depth of personality he has never plumbed, secretly craves the luxury he has been temporarily invited to enjoy. Marx talks Communism to two young ladies and thoroughly converts Ophelia, who falls in love with him. He, however, is oblivious to Ophelia's desire to learn more and more about the system, for he is busily learning to ride and hunt so that the object of his affections, Mary Springwheat, will fall in love with him. What he doesn't know is that Mary is already in love and has not a bit of interest in his learning the noble sports. True to her noble upbringing, however, she snubs him when he finally proffers his love; he soon leaves Woodmansterne; and Mary is left to regret her decision. After his initial conversations with Ophelia, he never approaches her again, for she is reading *Das Kapital* and becoming a bore. Marx, in the long run, is the only character in the book who truly develops.

The other characters are enveloped in varying degrees of stodginess, which, eventually, may be the very situation White is trying to depict. Nonetheless, they do not make for very interesting reading. Among others, there is a professor whose sole task is seemingly to stand for the opposite of what Marx represents; a writer, Timothy, who does not have nearly so much to say as we would expect from a writer so named; and various representatives of the upper English social class, each of whom possesses foibles which White always satirically exaggerates. The reader can only titter for so long at the Countess of Scamperdale's enumeration of her multifarious prejudices and at the Earl's reflections on the problems of his life while staring into a swirling commode.

The plot itself seems to divide into two halves. The first half is concerned with the group in each of its tedious daily activities; and White dutifully displays their stock reactions (based on rank and outlook) to each of them. There is a hunt early in the story in which White thoroughly ridicules all members, especially the women. Next follows a banquet, bringing with it the first discussion of Communism and the group's varying reactions to it. Then at night, when all the characters go to bed, they have their representative dreams—all except Marx who stays awake plotting the destruction of Woodmansterne and the entire British social order. The next chapter is breakfast—same pattern. After several chapters of the intellectual jokes that Sylvia Warner despises, there is another hunt, this one a bird hunt, in which not only pheasants but also several farm animals are killed. By the end of this hunt, several love affairs have begun; but, on the whole, most of the characters are boring each other as much as they are the reader. There is a general feeling that the hunt has been unsuccessful and the Earl even begins to worry about his status as a countryside gentry.

Various slapstick events begin at this time to enliven the story, if not to unify it. The Earl's children lock the visitors in a tower during a party, and they are stuck there for quite some time before the gardener discovers them. Later Ophelia is seduced; and the more righteous members of the group, assuming only a Communst would do such a thing, go to give Marx a well-deserved beating. The Professor, being a humanist above all, locks them in the kennels before they ever reach Marx. Marx himself is the subject of much humor as he fights furiously to stay on horseback and as he stays out long after dark to hunt the fox which he thinks will impress Mary Springwheat. Through it all, Marx's greatest adversary in the group, one Tiddly Holdhard, bears all the young man's boorishness in a festering anger. When, in the midst of the biggest of all the hunts, Marx hooks irons with Holdhard's mount as they jump a fence, it is more than the incensed Tiddly can stand: he advises Marx that he wants him to leave the country.

Under such pressures, the group eventually disperses, and the hunting vacation comes to a close. The local residents and traditional parasites, though, continue to hunt in an attempt to divert themselves. At this point, the very unexpected and rather forced ending takes place. One day when the Professor and Mary and several others are hunting near a local industrial town, Marx and Pansy Duquesne ride over to them to join the group. Before anyone can find out what the two outcasts are doing in the area, planes fly overhead and begin bombing the city and the surrounding environs. It seems that the hunting party is killed in the attack (and neither the reader nor White knows that they are not until they reappear in the sequel, *Gone to Ground*). Definitely eliminated, however, are the house and all the treasures at Woodmansterne, as well as the Earl of Scamperdale himself: "The Earl's own leg hung in a tree near Beding, swinging gently in the winter wind, but he and his progenitors stared down upon the ruin of their house in noble effigy"(251).[5]

White's satire in *Earth Stopped,* of course, deals, as he does so often, with the stagnation built into the British social system as a whole and into individuals in particular. The whole world seems to be motivated by a lust for personal gain, judging from the way the initially adamant Marx abandons his ideology so easily under the onslaught of wealth and libido. No character in the book seems to possess any sort of stable, admirable quality; each seems more adept at making a fool of himself than at any other more profitable skill. At the end, the ideologues of the left and the right, the Communists and the Fascists, are busily killing each other and the world; the silent middle is being strewn all over the countryside. The satire itself, as with the oversubtle jokes, is often too cute to be effective; when it is not too cute, it is too heavy—for example, the mass destruction and bloodshed at the end. Only one or two of the last hunting trips are presented nearly as well as White presents them in other books.

III Gone to Ground

Except possibly for the several nice reviews already mentioned in connection with *Earth Stopped,* it is difficult to determine what would force a man with White's talent and sensitivity to continue upon the same profitless lines he had tested in that novel. *Gone to Ground* uses the same characters (the ones who are still alive), saves them from the bomb which should by rights have killed them, finds them an underground dugout, and puts them in it to survive for at least ten days and possibly to found a new race of humans thereafter! Not only does White drag out the same characters, but he also places them in circumstances so unbelievable as to make them more unbearable than they were—if any human beings deserved to be bombed out of existence, the reader is tempted to feel, they were the ones.

At the risk of making White appear, in 1935 at least, very pragmatic and inartistic, it seems that the only reason *Gone to Ground* exists at all is to serve as a vehicle for many of his previously unpublished short stories. He has the stories narrated by the characters with whom he was most currently familiar and who had the best reasons for sitting down to tell relatively uninteresting and unexciting tales. Economically, for the struggling White, it was a book, as several of his other books were, which suddenly pieced itself together and which did not need the effort that a separately conceived novel would have required. Like some of the sporting diaries a book could be produced with a little patchwork.

The occasion of the stories is established, despite the fact that the world has been destroyed, with a comic-ironic tone, complete with coincidences which by themselves relieve and obscure the serious nature of the situation. Not only does the required dugout just happen to be there in the middle of a field just when it is needed, but the two owners also happen to be the father of the Countess of Scamperdale, Facey Romford, and the uncle of the Professor, Soapey Sponge. Though these two characters argue and bicker throughout the interludes between stories and appear relatively stupid in the tales they tell, we must at least give them credit for having run away from England and for having lived in the dugout for the primary purpose of escaping the boredom wrought by the Scamperdales and their friends.

The idea of a "sporting *Decameron*" is first suggested and developed by the garrulous professor, whose interminable stories are harder to repress as the days grow longer. Of the fourteen stories told, only a few are at all memorable. Almost all deal, appropriately, with the subjects of death or the supernatural; but White never relates the stories to each other thematically. Thus, in the long run no real statement is ever forthcoming about the nature of human extinction, the end of the world, or anything else.

Probably the finest story of all is the one told by the Countess in Chapter 10, the short tale called "The Spaniel Earl," which White had written some years before 1935. The Second Earl of Scamperdale, it seems, was so affected by cruelty to animals in his early youth that he soon assumed the characteristics of a dog. In the Countess's story, the family, worried at first, obtains for him a specially made kennel and a suit of fur clothing. This Swiftian fantasy, essentially a plotless series of vignettes, recounts various problems the boy had in attaining manhood or adult doghood or whatever. The central problem was finding a wife who would suit him and fulfill the requirements of extending the Scamperdale line. King Charles, who took a personal interest in this situation, had all the rulers of Europe comb their kingdoms for the right wife. They at first sought either virgins or bitches, but they later decided that only a combination of the two would satisfy the Spaniel Earl. After years of little luck, a girl is found who is reputed to be the offspring of a woman and a werewolf. She is brought to the Spaniel Earl, they satisfy each other, and they mate.

Many of the stories are pointless ghost stories—not even good representatives of a rather suspect genre. Others are dull hunting stories which the Professor now and then insists upon telling and which bore even the listeners in the dugout. One semi-philosophical tale is told by Sponge (of pilots and of the reason dynamic individuals commit suicide); a graphic horror story is narrated by Marx (about a professor who is really a troll and a wife-killer); another comic tale is told by Romford (about a sheepish husband named Timmy who tragically runs a pack of hounds through a yard in which his terrible wife breeds foxes); and a peculiarly twisted detective story is related by Pansy (wherein the world's greatest detective uses himself as bait to trap a murderer—and is killed). These four tales are the best in the collection. After the countess's story, the novel ends without fanfare. Romford leaves the dugout after ten days to see what the possibilities are for a new civilization—what he found we are never told. *Gone to Ground* concludes with another story by the Professor, and this one contains perhaps the ultimate point White is seeking to make. It is a disconnected tale of reverie in which the Professor eventually accuses himself of poaching fish. When discovered by the local keeper, he blusters his way through pedantic comments and questions before discovering the great love the keeper has for nature and the great insights he has into the natural order. The professor compares him to Pan. Before parting the keeper gives the Professor a small lesson in catching fish. Herein he stresses what is probably *Gone to Ground*'s ultimate moral: keep no living being doomed to die too long on the string—kill him quickly. As Romford and the rest wait to see what the new world will bring, White seems to be implying that they are like squirming fish, or, possibly a better analogy in this book, like a fox in a hole; they are waiting for the impossible escape that will allow contented existence once again. The absence of a stated answer is, of course, typical of White, for whom contented existence is not an alternative of the future.

IV England Have My Bones

England Have My Bones (1936) is the most difficult of all White's books to discuss, for its only unity is time and its real charm rests in its immediate expression, an element which obviously cannot be duplicated in a critical essay. This book, actually little more than one of White's daybooks rendered into polished prose, is the chronicle of his life between March 3, 1934, and the same day a year later. It deals centrally with his extraprofessional activities, namely shooting, flying, fishing, and fox-hunting; with one exception, these are the same activities he was to lambaste two years later in *Burke's Steerage* (1938). It is also the book which marks the beginning of the White-Garnett friendship. Having had an earlier novel somewhat favorably reviewed by Garnett,[6] White mailed him the manuscript of this book; and Garnett replied that he had found it enchanting. The review he eventually wrote for the *New Statesman*[7] called it a book of real power, though often tiresome; but other reviewers wholeheartedly approved of it. James Agate, in two antithetical sentences, expressed quite succinctly the reaction most readers have to it: "It is about subjects in which I am not even faintly interested. It is entrancing."[8]

The book definitely possesses its high and its low points. Because the reader of White has hunted and fished with him so many times in various volumes, the long central section about White's flying lessons is easily the most unique experience in *England Have My Bones*. There is a vividness here which, I would suspect, is extremely graphic even to those who have not known for themselves the oozy frustration of learning to pilot a plane. Mild catharses continually recur as White tries desperately to land his machine softly on the runway, only to experience instead splintering bounces on landings and wobbling twists on takeoffs. Quite often Faulkner's *Pylon* comes to mind as the reader of thirty-five years later watches a man entrust his life to a makeshift aircraft and to an irascible instructor. But flying, as well as the other three sports which the book treats, is an activity which is valuable for demonstrating the volume's only central thematic point: "Because I am afraid of things, of being hurt and death, I have to attempt them. This journal is about fear" (80).[9]

White began flying more or less on a dare, but he soon loved it. Not only did he join the local flying club after barely a half-hour in the sky, but also at one point early in his lessons he offered his instructor forty pounds for insurance if he would be allowed to fly solo at once. This desire, of course, was due to momentary exuberance; and, fortunately, White was not allowed to go. He did, however, pursue the lessons daily, having, as all potential pilots do, those moments of soft exhilaration and others of crunching frustration. Sitting behind the instructor, whose name was Johnny Burn, White learned to interpret by the color of his neck how he himself was doing. Working tirelessly to eliminate one bad habit, he would immediately replace it with another. When he had straightened out his takeoffs, he would then begin to fly with his right wing too low. Having picked up the wing, he would stall too high and land too hard. When the key moment came that Johnny said he would allow him to solo if he took one more good circuit of the field, White, in nervous anticipation, did everything wrong. The solo was postponed. On the next occasion that Johnny made this remark (this time he wanted two more good circuits), White landed with horrible bounces.

However, due to that strange intuition that only flight instructors seem to have, Johnny got out and the trembling author made one entire circuit of the field, alone and perfectly! White's remark on the occasion is one of the book's most memorable: "One's brain, which must always advocate the suicide's grave as the only reasonable solution, finds itself in conflict with one's vitality. I would recommend a solo flight to all prospective suicides. It tends to make clear the issue of whether one enjoys being alive or not" (136). In flying, White also gained one of his rare experiences of universal harmony—experiences he later records in three of his other journals:[10]

> Now came the nice part. It was lovely to be free. Against expectation, I am not lonely in an aeroplane. I wheeled and glided over the reservoirs and bathing lakes. Middlehampton was a pool of quicksilver towards the sun. Towns cease to be horrible when you are well above them. The other machines, coming in and going out, hung and crawled with beauty on the earth floor. (143)

In spite of frustration and several frightening moments, White continued to fly and was even contemplating autogyros by the book's conclusion.

The section on flight is the book's most extensive and most intriguing, due perhaps to several factors, not the least of which is the fact that it was the most intriguing for White. The final section on fox-hunting is the weakest, mainly because, as White himself states, this activity was one he found least enjoyable and least purposeful. The hunting and fishing sections are interesting at times, but White has written more compellingly about these elsewhere. *England Have My Bones* opens with a fishing trip to Aberdeen, which, despite the breakdown of his car, White recalls as one of life's most satisfying experiences. His fishing scout and tutor is a Scotsman named MacDonald, a far more patient man than the pilot Johnny. White thrills to his first salmon catch almost as much as to his first solo flight. During this fishing trip, however, he first begins to notice the difference between the true sportsman and the dilettante from London who participates because it seems the thing to do. He is repulsed by a Major Wynne, such a dabbler, who vies with him for MacDonald's assistance. Major Wynne, plus some of the people he will later encounter on the fox hunt, plant the seeds in his mind for his ill-received satire on noble sports, *Burke's Steerage.*

England Have My Bones is not, however, a four-part discussion of four activities. The four mesh with one another at various moments throughout the journal, and there are other topics included with them as well. In the midst of the highest enthusiasm for flying, there is a layman's discussion of types of clouds. For no other reason than that this episode occurs on a particular day, there is a treatment of water divining, obviously the roots of the hilarious lesson Mr. White gives Mikey on the subject in *The Elephant and the Kangaroo.* While sitting in a pub, White discusses the theory and scoring of an English dart game, complete with diagrams and recommendations for cheating to get the first throw. There are also, among others, discussions of trees, paintings, and dialects—all indicative of what Sylvia Warner has called a "jack-of-all-trades mind."[11]

As I remarked earlier in this discussion, *England Have My Bones* is a book whose merit rests mainly in its immediate and personal expression of a year of existence, and this virtue even a literary critic is not only unable but also loath to tamper with. This quality is particularly apparent in terms of several abstract discussions concerning the roles in life which most pleased White—author and sportsman. In the entry for September 21, 1934, White suddenly states his personal dissatisfaction about the book he has written:

> I suppose one has to be desperate, to be a successful writer. One has to reach a rock-bottom at which one can afford to let everything go hang. One has got to damn the public, chance one's living, say what one thinks, and be oneself. Then something may come out.
>
> But I am afraid to do this. I haven't the courage to chance starvation, and so I try to serve God and Mammon. I try to write "proper" books, which fizzle out for their propriety, when all the time there are other things that I should like to say and honester ways to say them. (211)

If he despairs of his art, he reassures us about the art of his sportsmanship, as he demonstrates in this definition of "killing":

> Killing is beginning to become clear to me. It came as an inspiration. Before, I had been puzzled at liking to kill things, because I am generally more humane than most people: certainly than the war-mongers, the flogging magistrates, the snake killers, and most school-masters. I cannot remember when I last killed a fly, or a wasp, or a mouse. It is, as I discovered yesterday, a question of art. When it is difficult to kill the thing, when skill and achievement come into it, I find that the killing is worthwhile. You forget the dead salmon in the ecstasy of creation: you have perfected something yourself, even more perfect than the dead fish. This must sound silly to anybody who has not shared the perfection; who has not created a cast, or a shot, or a run himself. But it is rock bottom. (259)

White, of course, varies from book to book in his view about the justifiability of killing living creatures, but this statement is one of his best about the sportsman's code.

England Have My Bones is one of the group of White's books which can still be easily bought; but it is not, I think, one of his better ones (nor is it one of his worst). A substantial amount of repetitiousness exists in any man's life, but too much of it is retained in this particular journal. For some reason, the reader identifies with White's agony in the heavy repetition in *The Goshawk*; but here the repetition, judging from White's ebullience throughout, seems to be the reader's agony alone. The chapters about flying are fine, probably because the factors of personal danger and personal fear (supposedly what the book is about) are the highest. The hunting, fishing, and shooting chapters tend to become tedious and perhaps would have been at times unbearable had it not been for the anecdotes and mild philosophizing which pervade them. But perhaps the dissatisfaction arises from the reader's tendency to read the book as he would a novel. The reviewer Agate suspected himself of such reading in 1936 when he remarked: "I wish I had time to read this book instead of having to review it. By 'reading' this book, I mean taking it in little doses, poring over it, having it by one's bedside, cherishing it."[12]

The book, finally, is one that is ironically framed. The first incident of note is the fact that, in Aberdeen, White cannot get his car to run. One year later he runs it into a ditch and temporarily blinds himself. More ironic still, however, is the fact that White participates in this volume's four major activities to challenge his fear of dying or being badly injured. He is challenging his fate, but his own carelessness nearly causes his death or maiming. In the final pages, therefore, he reprimands himself and all those who worry about and continually anticipate death; and he resolves to live henceforth in the present alone: "Like the animal and the great man, I prefer to live in the present: and not only prefer, but now . . . am actually contented. It is not necessary to choose. The great man is so" (357).

V Burke's Steerage

Though White himself called *Burke's Steerage* a "short, cheap thing,"[13] this work, subtitled *The Amateur Gentleman's Introduction to the Noble Sports and Pastimes,* is an ingenuously funny book.[14] Written to badger the Englishman about his three noble sports (fox-hunting, fishing, and shooting), White perhaps hit too low for English traditionalists, and the book consequently never reached a second printing. It is filled with humorous pen-and-ink sketches done by White himself which nicely complement the verbal satire he writes so well. Not a great book, it *is* genuinely entertaining.

The central figure in this satire, if indeed there really is one, is Amateur Gentleman, who, while never outwardly described, seems to be a young, middle-class comer who has "enough" (but not excessive) money to indulge in noble sports. Because he knows nothing about any of them, he is thus afraid of making a fool of himself in front of other people. Therefore, White's "manual" is devoted only very slightly to "sporting" expertly; the greater and the satiric bulk concerns "looking good even if you aren't." The tone of the book is one of under-the-table advice—something the Amateur Gentleman, White is sure, would love to have but would never care to pass around. Sports are not to be enjoyed—they are to be indulged in for reasons of social rank; therefore, face must at all times be saved.

The three sections of the book are parallel in content. The

opening chapter of each section is on "types"—types of fox-hunting, salmon fishing, and shooting. There are four of each, and each is wryly satiric. Fox-hunting, for example, can be either the *Leicestershire Hound* type (known only to cabinet members and rich Jews and indulged in more for the purpose of picture-taking than fox-hunting); the *Family Pack* type (in which local landowners band together against strangers and, even though they hate one another, hunt the fox "because no other course of action has ever occurred to them" [14])[15]; *The London Gentleman's* type (which is composed mostly of chattering city folk, who have neither met one another nor hunted foxes before); and the *God-Forsaken* type (a type to be scorned because it consists only of "farmers and low people like that" who wade through swamps and cut through forests for the "vulgar and unfashionable objective of catching foxes" [16]).

Fishing can be either *The Financier's* type (in the poor pools a businessman has purchased, at fifty thousand pounds apiece, for his own personal use); *The Laird's of That Ilk* type (in pools of unknown value because they have always been owned by noble families and, consequently, have never been fished); *The Hotel* type ("water of known inferiority which is fruitlessly flogged by such members of the rising bourgeoisie who cannot get their noses in anywhere else" [65]); or *Worm Water* (where, in 1881, an old gentleman fishing for trout caught a salmon and which has, therefore, lured sportsmen back fruitlessly year after year). Shooting is also of four kinds: the *Certain Personage* type (in which a nobleman fills the bushes with hired shooters to bring down a bevy of fowl every time he fires his own gun; *The Family* type (where, in quest of family unity and pleasure, parents and children alike shoot at anything that moves, and often, by mistake, at each other); the *Syndicate* type (in which a group of avid hunters bands together at their financed lodge on Sunday afternoons to shoot and to be duped and robbed the other six days of the week by their trusty caretaker); or, finally, the *Farmer's Glory* type (in which, strange as it may seem, a group of farmers get together to shoot for sport and relaxation after the harvest has been reaped). On the basis of those which are "in," expert White recommends to the Amateur Gentleman which type to participate in and which to avoid.

The second chapter in each section attempts to analyze "reasons" for partaking in each sport: fox-hunting (to prove one is not "chicken"), fishing (because man is actually a psychological iceberg, more beneath the surface of the water, symbolic for the unconscious, than above it), and shooting (which White is afraid to reflect upon, though he feels it results from "an unsatisfactory married life" [112]). From reasons which, we note, always lack love for a particular sport or a general sporting interest, White proceeds to "correct costume," emphasizing the absolute necessity for a red coat in fox-hunting, an eccentric hat in fishing, and proper boots in shooting. Then he presents a list of purchases which the Amateur Gentleman will be expected to make, not to ensure success in his chosen sport, but, again, to save face at it. White in fact emphasizes that the people who catch the most fish are those with a branch and a piece of cord—but they do not *look good*—the primary consideration. The cost of looking good, of course, runs into thousands, but this expense must be defrayed.

In White's discussion of etiquette, a topic in which, especially in the case of fox-hunting and shooting, we discover some of the book's most humorous material. On shooting, for instance, White is, as he is throughout *Burke's Steerage,* intent and matter of fact: "The Chief etiquettes in shooting are connected with the lives of human beings and with the lives of those creatures which they intend to kill. Both lives are assumed to be valuable: that of the creature because if it is not alive you cannot kill it, and that of the human being for reasons much less logical and possibly quite fallacious" (120–21).

After describing all the procedures involved in etiquette in face-saving terminology, White attempts to picture the average day of the average fox-hunter, fisherman, and fowler—a picture which demonstrates that all are involved in attempting to save face at the expense of everyone else. The fox-hunt is especially graphic, particularly about what happens when all the riders converge on the one low point of an otherwise insurmountable fence:

The holes are quickly adopted by those in front of us, and, by the time we get there, there are four queues waiting to jump at the four gaps. All the members of these queues are cursing each other feverishly, some exclaiming: "Damn you, can't you give me room to jump?" Others: "Damn you, don't jump in front of me." Others: "Damn you, don't jump behind me." And others more simply: "Damn you."

It is our turn now . . . and here we go over the few remaining twigs, not very gracefully but safely, amid a shower of damns. (56)

The fisherman, who gulps down his breakfast in order to be first one in the river (but leaves his equipment in the kitchen), and the shooter, who fires sixty-five times and brings down one and a half birds, have equally ludicrous "average" days.

The parallelism of the book's three sections is satirically employed, therefore, to mock the "noble sports and pastimes." In fact, the structure is violated only twice: White pauses, between "equipment" and "etiquette," to discuss what a fox hunter should pay for the privilege of fox-hunting (again dictated by "face-saving" since what one pays is listed in an annual yearbook); later, between "etiquette" and "an average day," he digresses for a few serious remarks about the subject of "Sport." Some of these comments, whether they were intended satirically or not, are well stated:

It is the instinct, the instinct to back oneself against difficulties, which is the basis of all sports. The fisherman finds that it is relatively easy to catch trout on the worm, so he handicaps himself (increases the difficulty which has to be overcome) by determining to catch trout on a hook ornamented with a piece of rubber tube in the likeness of a worm. The slayer of foxes becomes bored by murdering them with a gun, so he expends eight thousand pounds a year in training dogs to do it in a much more complicated manner. The shooter, able to butcher any number of sitting rabbits by creeping up to them while they are feeding in the evening, stands up and waves his arms to make them run.

. . . The horrible realisation [of destroying a beautiful animal] will soon be dulled by custom, *provided that in destroying that beauty he can at the same time congratulate himself upon having created another beauty, the beautiful shot.* (50)

For White this distinction seems to be the differentiation between simple killing and sport, a matter his conscience often debated both in private and in print.

Though White did not like the way his book was written—it was too facile and imitative, he felt—and though his offended public bought very few copies, *Burke's Steerage* is—to a reader thirty years later and of another country—a worthwhile, enjoyable book.

CHAPTER 4

The Once and Future King

I The Sword in the Stone

THE *Sword in the Stone* (1938) is the first novel in the tetralogy upon which White's fame eventually rests, and it had its roots in an essay White had written some years earlier about the impracticalities inherent in Thomas Malory's version of the King Arthur legend. To this base White added various hunting myths and an occasional philosophical passage; however, the satire, both Arthurian and contemporary, dominates the book. Read by itself, the novel is light and refreshing; considered as the first book in the tetralogy, it is contrapuntally ominous.

The narrative of *The Sword and the Stone* is divided structurally into two parts. During the first nineteen chapters, the main character, Wart (who is, of course, later to be King Arthur) learns the knack of being a young gentleman in a rather unconventional way. In the last five chapters (whose events occur six years after the first nineteen), he moves from his position of noble nobody to discover that he is the rightful heir to Uther Pendragon's throne. The first part of the story is extremely episodic, though White probably had no choice if he were to fulfill his initial purpose of satirizing the components of the Arthurian legend. Wart and Kay are taught how to do all the conventional things knights do, though Wart seems to be just an observer—Kay alone is to be Sir Ector's heir. Thus, while Wart is all eyes and ears, feeling extremely privileged to be part of it all, Kay is continually smug, assuming that his birthright will eventually permit him to learn knighthood by osmosis. The magician Merlyn, whose character bears none of the sinister aspects of some of the other Arthurian tales, befriends Wart;

for, living backwards in time as he does, he knows Wart's ultimate destiny, both its successes and its tragic conclusion.

Merlyn, who is about the only character in the book not fooled by all the chivalric incidents in the kingdom (he has lived, after all, in the age of the electric light and the *Encyclopaedia Britannica*), tries to tolerate such things as King Pellinore and his Questing Beast; but he really regards them with a jaundiced eye. Even poor Wart, who knows he is supposed to respect the traditional values and activities, eventually can do nothing but scratch his head about what he sees. To afford Wart a true "eddication," however, Merlyn steals him away from his daily lessons in useless knowledge to school him in the ways of nature and of the world. He periodically transforms him into various animals—a fish, hawk, ant, owl, wild goose, badger—all animals the magician feels have lessons to teach. Some of the book's most satiric and philosophical passages are contained in episodes in which Wart is not in possession of his own body. Throughout these passages, the reader is never sure whether White intends the boy to be dreaming such fantastic events or actually experiencing them; however, evidence seems to point to the latter. Wart, however, is afforded an opportunity during these years for *normal* Arthurian adventures as well. From these he learns equally as much in terms of human compassion and love—the Robin Hood escapades and the boar hunt are some of the more memorable.

Not until Chapter 20 does the novel develop a progressive plot line. In this chapter the death of Uther Pendragon is announced; and the contest of the sword in the anvil is devised. Sir Kay, who is about to be knighted, decides that the festivities in London would provide a proper setting for an event of such universal significance as his dubbing; therefore, he, his squire (Wart), and the whole entourage from Sir Ector's palace journey there. On the day Kay is to fight in his first tournament, his excitement causes him to leave his sword in his hotel room; and he orders Wart to get it. Wart, furious and disgruntled about being commanded by a young man heretofore his companion and his equal, does what he is told; but when he finds the hotel door locked, he spies a sword in an anvil, removes it with some difficulty, and returns to Kay. Kay, who recognizes the sword immediately, proclaims that he removed it from its hold; but, upon being questioned by Ector, he admits his lie. Wart (after demonstrating over and over again that he can pull the sword out and after letting every other wretch in town have a chance to try to do so) is proclaimed King Arthur. The story ends in festivity; but Merlyn, knowing what is to happen (for him it already *has* happened), quietly plans to leave Arthur forever.[1]

White, of course, has felt no compulsion to remain true to anything in the traditional Arthurian legend which did not suit his fancy. Uther and Arthur, both Normans, live in the twelfth century; but most datings place Arthur's mythological (or real?) reign many centuries earlier and most afford him a Celtic heritage. At any rate, White seems to have replaced William the Conqueror with Uther, since the latter's reign also began in 1066. The assimilation of the Robin Hood material with that about King Arthur is also not usually done. Certainly Robin Hood never was named Robin Wood, as he and his friends insist in this novel that they were. Even the dignity of the removal of the sword from the stone is rendered in haphazard circumstances in the White version; but this change is obviously congruent with the author's attempt to poke fun at all the hoopla and commotion that Malory so relished in his version.

The satire in the novel assumes two forms. On the one hand, there is the type for which Walt Disney paid a miniscule amount of cash for the movie rights—knights' falling off horses because their armor is too heavy, and the like, all of which the motion picture producer saw as great cartoon material. The other satire is more Swiftian—the human race itself is taken to task for universal but correctable faults. Among these faults, of course, is the theory that Might is Right; and this concept is the fault Arthur tries unsuccessfully to overcome throughout the next three volumes. With this more serious satire we will concern ourselves.

The frame satire—the one which encompasses the more minor and diverse ones—of the entire novel deals with the subject of human worth and inherited rank, something which bothered White enough to write about it in several books. The contrast is initially established in Chapter 1 where Kay and Wart are quickly compared. At first, White seems to be dealing in traditional good-guy, bad-guy separation; but this impression is soon and effectively dissolved. Kay, in the opening chapter, appears to be negative—he loses at sports, does a sloppy job in the hay-making, bears standard prejudices, and relies on class distinction and his own birthright. In the second chapter, he shirks his duty by leaving Wart to search all night for a falcon they have lost while he himself retires to his bed. Later, Kay kills birds just when Merlyn and Wart have established bestial nobility; and he claims to have pulled Excalibur from the stone just when Wart proved his claim to the kingdom. Yet Kay performs well in the rescue of Wat, the Dog Boy, and of Friar Tuck from Morgan Le Fay; and, at another time, he sincerely craves the knowledge Merlyn is so freely disseminating to Wart.

Early in the novel White makes it clear that Kay is not a villain—he is merely an unextraordinary human being: "He was not at all an unpleasant person really, but clever, quick, proud, passionate and ambitious. He was one of those people who would be neither a follower nor a leader, but only an aspiring heart, impatient in the failing body which imprisoned it" (34–35).[2] In some ways the book might be, in a slight way, Kay's tragedy in itself; for, as Merlyn predicts for him on this same occasion, " 'Kay . . . thou wast ever a proud and ill-tongued speaker, and a misfortunate one. Thy sorrow will come from thine own mouth' " (34). And the sorrow seems to have been created, when all is said and done, by the environment in which Kay is placed by fate—an environment which cultivates pride in selected members and allows it to evaporate at the very moment the cultivated character must depend upon it—as it does for Kay when he lies about having pulled the sword from the stone.

Wart, for several reasons, all of which are denied to poor Kay, overcomes the environment. Most basically, born in a lower position, he has less opportunity to succumb to the environment than Kay. Next, he has Merlyn; and Merlyn, knowing that Kay is socially a nobody, concentrates entirely upon England's unknowing but future monarch. When Merlyn converts Wart into animals and when Wart attempts a display of pride and social status with these lower beings, he experiences catharsis after catharsis. Making Wart see the natural intelligence of lower species and the almost natural folly of mankind is Merlyn's main and most difficult task. Enamored of knights and fighting, Wart is unable to see the stupidity in what King Pellinore and Sir Grummore are doing when they conflict. He is so used to the fact that men periodically make war upon one another that he thinks the animals who do not are somewhat unstable. His progressive realization of all the hopeless inequities eventually causes him to begin thinking about the Might-is-Right philosophy that he is to debate and resist (unsuccessfully) during the rest of his life.

Though the novel is far from metaphysical, the nature of man is either directly or obliquely discussed continually. One of the novel's most memorable passages is the parable of the embryos about which the wise badger tells Wart in the twenty-first chapter. In the story, God, in speaking to the embryos at the moment of Creation, offered each species some gift which it thought would help it endure life on earth. Most of the animals asked for the characteristics for which they are best known today, but man's embryo delayed in making a request. When asked why, the embryo replied that whatever God, of His own will, chose to give it must be right. In reward for his faith and foresight, God made man the most blessed of all animals by allowing him a multitude of practical traits. According to the badger, though, man has misused these many gifts to make himself also the most dominant and powerful animal. Man, as an extension of these gifts, has voluntarily made war upon his fellows.

Though some have called White misanthropic, he is attempting to demonstrate that man is essentially good but possesses power he has not yet learned to properly channel or to control. The power to love has become secondary to the power to overcome. The chapters on the ants and the geese (both later additions which were supposed to have been included in the planned fifth volume of the set, *The Book of Merlyn*) discuss the nature of war, but they do so more in terms of its folly and hideousness than in consideration of the primal instincts that perpetrate it. The first thing that Wart notices after Merlyn has turned him into an ant is the number of dead bodies in the colony. In the satire on the ants, the reader observes a condemnation of the ant-human psychology in general and of the then current German Fascism in particular. Ants, Wart finds, do not think anything out in advance—they act spontaneously. Ants never stop to enjoy life—they work constantly, always striving for greater material gain than they have yet amassed. In addition to these qualities, they have an irrational respect for their Hitler-like leader, whose only job it is to lay eggs and broadcast orders. For an ant to ask a question about his existence is to demonstrate punishable insanity. The most Juvenalian comparison White manages in the chapter is the remark that only six species make war upon or kill other members of the same species—five are breeds of ants; the sixth is the human race. Just as war is breaking out in the ant colony, Merlyn changes Wart back to his human form.

The chapter on geese (18) is more Horatian and somewhat repetitive. Recognizing Wart as an outsider, one female befriends the new goose and "shows him the ropes" of this particular society. When Wart, at one point, notices the sentries posted around the flock, he asks if the geese are at war. The concept of war is so foreign to the female that she cannot comprehend his question. Instead, she indicates that sentries are only needed (naturally!) for defense against other species, never against their own. When Wart volunteers that fighting one another can be a lot of fun, she bluntly classifies him as a baby—and the badger does, too, three chapters later. The geese passage also brings the subject of monarchy into the discussion. Among the geese no leader is ever chosen as one must, it seems, be chosen among men. The "leader" is the man (or bird) who demonstrates the greatest skill and leadership ability; he is not, as among men, the man with the fated birthright or the greatest Might. The procedure is reminiscent of the Germanic *comitatus,* which is evident in several medieval works of literature.

Throughout the novel, then, man is either being directly or obliquely satirized, and the satire invariably connects itself, as it always must, to some philosophical position that the author either forthrightly or indirectly expresses. White's philosophy, it seems to me, roots itself in the concept of education. The training Kay is given in Sir Ector's castle should not be regarded as a satire about medieval customs alone but more directly as one about the general irrelevance of "acceptable knowledge." Kay learns jousting and knightly tradition in the same way a modern student learns baseball and history. White would consider such skills of both ages to be of tertiary value, for they seem to be unassimilated bulks of material which have no relationship to the human being whose brain they are clogging and whose vision they are clouding. Rather, the alternative White offers is Merlyn's insistence that Wart be schooled in the ways of Nature, that his textbooks be experience, and that his homework be the development of self-reliance. The chapter in which Merlyn explains this philosophy to Wart becomes slightly Emersonian, as the terminology obviously is, before it concludes. Merlyn's prime virtue throughout the book is his oneness with Nature, to the extent that he can convert Wart into any animal, that he can speak with all, that he can heal the wounds of any. Merlyn is regarded as queer by the folk at Ector's for this very reason, just as are Wat and the Dog-Boy, who have rejected the "civilization" and unnatural pursuits of the castle and have withdrawn from it forever. White implies that Wart's discovery of true natural behavior (and nothing else) finally enables him to pull the sword from the stone. At this moment, in fact, all the creatures Wart has come to know throughout his life are present to give him directions about extricating the weapon.

Running concurrently with this philosophy of life, however, is the admission by both White and his spokesman Merlyn that the world seems constantly to be prohibiting the actualization of such a philosophy. Though Emerson and Thoreau fail to notice the fact, one man's right attitude can seldom overcome the wrong ones of the masses. In the rest of this tetralogy, Arthur discovers this truth more and more as he attempts to channel the Might available to him and the men of his Round Table toward some constructive end, only to have petty selfishnesses, his own and that of others, continually channel it back to the cursed philosophy of Might is Right. Even in Arthur's young life, as portrayed in the present novel, Wart frequently slips back to all-too-human behavior, as when he intimidates a hedgehog after being turned into a badger late in the book. His mind also gravitates frequently toward the traditional love of fighting and the proving of one's superior strength. White seems to be implying, as it would be current to do, that every man has within him a potential Hitler-complex; and, thus, the satire he launches against the rising German and his people is more universal that it at first appears.

As we have mentioned, White is fatalistic about overcoming such a behavior in mankind as a whole. When Arthur eventually tries to do so, he is swamped by it. Yet Merlyn believes that limited success is available to one man alone. In the novel's most famous, most beautiful, and most often-quoted passage, Merlyn instructs Wart on the method of alleviating the sadness which is a result of not being allowed all one feels he ought to be in life:

> "The best thing for being sad," replied Merlyn, beginning to puff and blow, "is to learn something. That is the only thing that never fails. You may grow old and trembling in your anatomics, you may lie awake at night listening to the disorder of your veins, you may miss your only love, you may see the world about you devastated by evil lunatics, or know your honour trampled in the sewers of baser minds. There is only one thing for it then—to learn. Learn why the world wags and what wags it. That is the only thing which the mind can never exhaust, never alienate, never be tortured by, never fear or distrust, and never dream of regretting. Learning is the thing for you. Look at what a lot of things there are to learn—pure science, the only purity there is. You can learn astronomy in a lifetime, natural history in three, literature in six. And then, after you have exhausted a milliard lifetimes in biology and medicine and theocriticism and geography and history and economics—why, you can start to make a cartwheel out of the appropriate wood, or spend fifty years learning to begin to learn to beat your adversary at fencing. After that you can start again on mathematics, until it is time to learn to plough." (185–86)

Although this passage recommends that man escape the unnatural concerns of the world for the real and important ones, Merlyn admits that few are able to do so, even if they sincerely want to. And he seems to attribute this incapability to the jaundiced eye of age which robs the idealistic youth of his good intentions and replaces them with a self-devouring desire to make himself comfortable in his old age.[3] This, again, Wart, as King Arthur, discovers when he realizes that he is ignoring the indiscretions of Lancelot and Guenever in order to maintain the harmony of his kingdom.[4]

Some critics have claimed that the tone of *The Sword in the Stone* is too light to support the growing tragedy of the tetralogy's last three books; but a closer examination demonstrates that, amid all the comedy and light satire, there is a serious and dark message underlying the deceptive façade of this book. The reader laughs at the pigeons who have a "parlement" and make laws for themselves, but White (and Chaucer) realize the underlying implication of a race of beings with sufficient moral integrity to allow their consciences to be their sole guides. The continual (and laughable) satire of the type of thing Ector's court holds important is merely a disguise for the very real fact that these people ignore, in the process, the very crucial moral issues of human existence. The scene in which the hawks prepare their military brigades should be regarded as a mirror image for much of the mindlessness and irrationality which has directed mankind's military efforts throughout history. When England heaps hoards of useless gifts upon Arthur at his coronation, White is definitely peeping around the corner at the hungry faces which have foregone their food so that the heaping and hoarding tradition might be continued. When Pellinore and Grummore fight, the situation is hilarious; but the fact that they feel that, at the very sight of each other, they *must* fight is horrifying. The fact that Pellinore must pursue the Questing Beast rather than consider the more important questions of life is truly amusing only at the first glance. All of these inconsistencies are so oblique on White's part that he leaves the reader with a fairy tale on the *first* reading and with a major satire and demand for reconsideration of human existence on the *second.*

A consideration of *The Sword in the Stone* cannot be terminated without noting the presence of White himself within the novel. I am quite certain that he saw himself in both Merlyn and Wart—the man who thought more about daily existence and its ultimate meaning than most of his contemporaries and the boy who could never learn enough to place the entire human experience, in its multitudinous forms, in a unified perspective. As a result, his two heroes are, respectively, men with a tragic sensitivity and a tragic end. Such figures are present in many White books, especially the later ones.[5]

The distinction between Merlyn and Wart should be ignored, I think, in evaluating White's own presence in the novel, for the ability of Merlyn to make Wart into a badger and Wart's actually being a badger are a unified product of White's imagination. If we add the dimension of experience to the imagination, much of what happens to Wart becomes extremely realistic and believable. In the eighteenth chapter, for example, Archimedes, Merlyn's owl, teaches Wart (now a bird) to fly—and the lesson resembles greatly the diary of flying that White included in the earlier book *England Have My Bones.* When the dog Beaumont dies on the boar hunt in the sixteenth chapter, the reader is given an insight into the decade-long anticipation that White endured of the eventual death of Brownie.[6] In the chapter dealing with the hawks, White is surely trying to see (as he did at the time of its occurrence) the whole process of the life and training of a goshawk from the animal's point of view. In addition to this mixture of imagination and experience, there is also, as there always is in a White book, a large amount of pure imaginative reflection—such as the "fruity taste like eating a peach with the skin on" (162) that Wart experiences when he eats the magic mouse which will turn him into an owl.

In addition to this imaginative, experiential dimension, *The Sword in the Stone* also contains many references to the various sports White loved; but most of these allusions are to people who improperly pursue them, such as Kay's killing birds simply because of his boredom with shooting at inanimate targets. Master Twyti chases boars only because he is a paid boar-chaser. As a result, anyone who has read much of White's work can easily contrast these situations to the many statements about the true rationales behind sports and hunting that White provides in countless other places.[7] Beyond sports, though, the novel also delves into some of White's most esoteric (and perhaps most incompetent) areas of endeavor—in Chapter 17, there is a serious, though rather inept, consideration of the origins of language.

Some of this material—like the study of linguistics—tends to disunify the book; but most concerns, unlike those in many other White books, are very coherently included and seldom smack of mere intellectual snobbery.

The Sword in the Stone is indeed rich in satire, in nonperipatetic philosophy, in comedy, and in a somewhat opinionated re-creation of an age. Its most masterful component, however, is its tone, which is constantly in tension between the lighthearted approach of a boy learning about the world he lives in and the tragic gloom that builds in the later books to the ultimate destruction of the boy's ideals. It is a book, thus, of genuinely mass appeal—the young read it as an ingenious adventure story; the old, as cathartic reflection on the unrealized potentialities of all men. The general reader finds in it a colorful panorama of life and its daily problems; the scholar sees it as a sensitive man's reaction to an existence he finds ultimately fatalistic. The book is both a comedy and a tragedy; and it is both a self-contained novel and a mere foundation for the three other books that follow it. White's single greatest achievement, this book, is most representative of the peculiar talent he possessed.

II The Queen of Air and Darkness

Originally titled *The Witch in the Wood,* the second book of the Arthurian tetralogy was begun even before *The Sword in the Stone* had been released by the publishers. White had completed the greater part of the second novel before the close of 1938; and, when he took it with him on a fishing trip to Ireland in February, 1939, he intended to finish it within two weeks' time. He took a room at a farmhouse (called "Doolistown") in County Mayo and did not finish the book until May 5. Much of the material for the novel itself seems to have been first gathered during this brief period (notably, the constant satire upon the Catholic religion and Irish civilization) as well as the early inspiration for two later books, *The Elephant and the Kangaroo* (about his life with the McDonaghs) and *The Godstone and the Blackymor* (about Irish tradition). White found the conditions for composition so tolerable, in fact, that he remained at Doolistown for six years after the completion of *The Witch in the Wood.*

White delivered the manuscript in late May to Collins, but within a short time they returned it to White. The publishers had discovered what White and his friend Potts secretly already knew—that the central female character of the book, Morgause, Arthur's half-sister, was in actuality White's mother who had come alive in the novel as a hated person rather than a hateful character. After Potts had severely reprimanded his friend for the multicastrations his mother had performed upon him in his literary efforts, White grimly rewrote parts of the novel, and he found doing so quite a chore since he was already thinking about the Lancelot volume and since he also despised redoing what he had thought already done. The result was a less-than-satisfactory revision; but Collins accepted the novel and issued it in April, 1940.

This series of incidents is quite important to White's final product, *The Once and Future King.* Realizing the need to rework *The Witch in the Wood* and concurrently feeling compelled to push forward on *The Ill-Made Knight,* White produced works with which he was not satisfied. *The Witch in the Wood* was loosely structured, and Morgause had fallen too far from view; *The Ill-Made Knight* showed signs of divided attention. Several years later, when preparing for the publication of the tetralogy in one volume, White wanted to revise both novels in order to make them fit better with the fourth book (and a possible fifth). Collins recoiled from the cost of resetting all the type; and, though Collins was the eventual publisher of the full work (generally unrevised), White thereafter took all his business to Jonathan Cape.

The Queen of Air and Darkness (formerly titled, until 1958, *The Witch in the Wood*) is easily a less perfect book than *The Sword in the Stone*; but in terms of White's dominant themes, it is more explicit and less elusive. The first book was the story, episodic in nature, of a young boy who learns the "right" things by day and the real things from Merlyn by night. White obscured the central purpose with an enormous amount of comedy and satire directed at the Arthurian legend. *The Queen of Air and Darkness* is not so difficult to analyze, for it is far more directly philosophic and potentially tragic. While it simultaneously maintains the jibes at chivalry, Irish Catholicism, and the pursuit of the Questing Beast, it contains more detailed debates about the questions of war, death, and motherhood. Once again, the tone continually shifts, but the tenor has now swung toward a consideration of the impending doom in Arthur's life, even though Arthur is still a relatively young man.

The novel is structurally confused. The central character in the first and last chapters is Morgause, Arthur's half-sister, who is planning in the beginning something mysterious and is carrying it out at the conclusion—the planting of the seeds of doom for Arthur's kingdom. Thus, Morgause's actions and intentions, as diluted as her character is by the rewriting of the novel, still form the frame of the story; and everything within the novel must be evaluated in terms of the shadow her existence casts upon it. Such an evaluation is often difficult for the reader to make, but Merlyn, at least, continually chews his beard in worry. The material found within the frame is generally divided into three categories—the discussions of Arthur and Merlyn, the "pranks" of Morgause's sons, and the pursuit by Pellinore, Grummore, and Palomides of the Questing Beast (or, later, her pursuit of them).

In order to sustain a minor degree of mystery and suspense about the real identity of Wart in the first Arthurian novel, White was forced to omit consideration of the opening books of Malory, the books in which Arthur's somewhat confused lineage is established; but including this material becomes his first task in the second novel. Omitting Malory's omniscient approach, White has Morgause's four sons—Gawaine, Agravaine, Gaheris, and Gareth—recount Arthur's heritage among themselves for their own enjoyment or education. Spiced with a homey touch or two (they refer to Igraine and the Duke of Tintagil as "Granny" and "Granda"), their account is faithful to Malory's version. Uther Pendragon, King of England, became attracted to Igraine, the wife of his enemy, the Duke of Tintagil, a Cornish duke (whom White calls the Earl of Cornwall). Uther Pendragon invites them to his castle, hoping to dishonor Igraine; but, when she discovers his treachery before he can take advantage of her, she and her husband run and lock themselves in two castles: Igraine, in the Castle Tintagil; the Duke, in the Castle Terrabil. After killing her husband, Uther forces

Igraine "into marrying him." The Malory version of seduction, one in which Uther assumes the countenance of the Duke, is omitted because of the young ages of the tellers—they do not yet understand such things. Because of Uther's misuse of their grandmother, the four boys have a sworn hatred for Arthur, whom they refer to as MacPendragon; and they have a sensitive loyalty to their mother and her sisters Elayne and Morgan Le Fay, whom they consider innocent victims of circumstance. Thus, the Arthurian legend is virtually intact; but White, as is his custom throughout the tetralogy, now proceeds to investigate the behavioral patterns of the people involved rather than banish them to genealogical tables as Malory is content to do in the early pages of his work.

Arthur, always very impressive and very impersonal in the early books of Malory, is considerably improved by White. He is, in fact, very human—to use White's words "he had fair hair and a stupid face" (225).[8] The stupid face seems White's way of saying that Arthur, though adept at yanking swords out of anvils, is still not so well trained as a king might be in the real, less-than-glamorous duties of his office. For Merlyn, Arthur's fox-hunt approach to warfare, for example, is totally frightening. Henceforth, from the first mention of the subject in Chapter 2, the legality and the morality, as well as the means and the ends, of warfare become the most important theoretical question the novel considers.[9] In the course of the discussions, Arthur's face changes from stupid to idealistic—it becomes so idealistic, in fact, that Merlyn is dismayed each time Arthur conceives a new opinion.

Written in the year when Hitler was first threatening England, *The Queen of Air and Darkness* clearly draws heavily upon White's personal reflections during this period about his own duty to join or avoid the British armed forces.[10] The subject is initially brought up by the King's off-hand remark to Merlyn that his victory over Lot was " 'a jolly battle . . .it was fun' " (227). To Arthur, the fight seems even more "jolly" since only commoners were killed—all the knights, except one with a broken leg, were still intact. Merlyn, who is angered, points out that Arthur and most so-called chivalrous kings actually base their entire approach to ruling upon an uncomplicated, time-worn, convenient Might-Is-Right philosophy. Whoever can order more "little men" into battle is entitled to the victory and to the accompanying spoils. Arthur, who seems until now to have forgotten his boyhood training, is quick to recognize the injustice but much slower in proposing a solution. In the memorable scene which closes this initial debate about the Might-Is-Right philosophy, Arthur takes his first small step toward conceiving the Utopian Camelot he proposes late in this novel and tries vainly to protect in the two following ones. Looking over the castle wall, he sees a servant carrying buckets from the menagerie; and he muses upon what it would be like to kill a man by dropping a small stone on his head from a great height:

> "I have never killed anybody like that," said the boy, in an inquisitive tone.
>
> Merlyn was watching.
>
> "You are the King," he said.
>
> Then he added, "Nobody can say anything to you if you try."
>
> Arthur stayed motionless, leaning out with the stone in his hand. Then, without his body moving, his eyes slid sideways to meet his tutor's.
>
> The stone knocked Merlyn's hat off as clean as a whistle, and the old gentleman chased him featly down the stairs, waving his wand of lignum vitae. (230)

In this small incident Arthur is morally convinced that Might is *not* Right.

This episode by no means ends the discussion. The King and the magician periodically continue to mull over the problem of war, and they eventually wonder if Might might not be employed to bring about right. First, though, they present a brief analysis of how individual wars—particularly the one with the Gaelic confederation in which they are presently engaged—get started.[11] Merlyn suggests racial history—that, hard as it is to believe, peoples continue to fight other peoples for centuries after the initial perpetrators have passed away; and he uses the conflict between the Normans and the Saxons as a good example. Arthur and Kay are astounded at this seeming senselessness; and, after discovering that the present war was initially provoked by his own father against the Gaels, Arthur is loathe to fight it. He even suggests abdicating—an indication that his idealism is developing rapidly.

This desire to eliminate the Might-Is-Right approach to kingship is, essentially, the very cornerstone upon which Camelot, in the future years, is built. When Arthur suggests to Merlyn that all war is immoral, Merlyn more wisely replies: " 'No. There is one fairly good reason for fighting—and that is, if the other man starts it' " (237). (With precisely this reason heretofore conscription-dodger White finally convinced himself to attempt to join the British forces in World War II—Hitler had started it.) The "starter" of a war is not hard to discover—he is the man who strikes the first blow; there is no justifiable reason for anyone to *start* a war, for " 'the wicked thing about a war is its beginning' " (237). This wickedness is precisely why, decides Merlyn, that the biggest disagreement in any war is who started it. At the conclusion of this conversation, which encompasses two full chapters (3 and 4), Arthur has changed from his war-as-sport viewpoint (" 'in which the poor man will be the only one who dies' ") of the traditional medieval noble (according to Merlyn) to right-and-wrong warfare in which the only determinant is whether or not one has struck the first blow—if one has, one is *wrong*; if one has not, one is *right* in fighting.

The question's facile answer becomes more difficult just prior to the Battle of Bedegraine in which Arthur again fights the Gaels. The following dialogue of Arthur with himself demonstrates why:

"Well, I was talking to Merlyn on the battlements one day, and he mentioned that the last battle we had—in which seven hundred kerns were killed—was not so much fun as I had thought it was. Of course, battles are not fun when you come to think about them. I mean, people ought not to be killed, ought they? It is better to be alive."

"Very well. But the funny thing is that Merlyn was helping me to win battles. He is still helping me, for that matter, and we hope to win the battle of Bedegraine together, when it comes off."

"We will," said Sir Ector, who was in on the secret.

"That seems to me to be inconsistent. Why does he help me to fight wars, if they are bad things?"

There was no answer from anybody, and the King began to speak with agitation.

"I could only think," said he, beginning to blush, "I could only think that I—that we—that he—that he wanted me to win them for a reason."

He paused and looked at Merlyn, who turned his head away.

"The reason was—was it?—the reason was that if I could be the master of my kingdom by winning these two battles, I could stop them afterwards and then do something about the business of Might. Have I guessed? Was I right?"

The magician did not turn his head, and his hands lay still in his lap.

"I was!" exclaimed Arthur. (253)

The ability to harness Might *for* Right is henceforth the tetralogy's major question; and Arthur obviously feels that, could he but win two more battles, the old order—represented by Lot and Uriens—which caters to the whims of nobility with no regard for justice would be totally eliminated and replaced by a better one. Yet, even in these noble sentiments, Arthur begins to sow the seeds of Fascism which White knows first motivated Hitler and every other tyrant the world has known. He plans to institute a "chivalric order" which everyone would be forced to join and would even consider it an honor to be part of. It would dedicate itself to using Might *for* Right and inspire its adherents to venture forth on crusades that would both assist the oppressed and vent their own combative energies. Ultimately its noble goal is to turn bad into good; but, like all imposed Orders, "good" is internally and relatively and often ignobly defined. Merlyn, who, we must remember, lives backward in time, has already known countless men with such ideals of using Might to create Right; and, when Arthur seeks his comment, Merlyn can only remain sadly and dutifully silent.[12] When Kay later expresses a similar position—that war is essentially to eliminate the stupidity of those who refuse to see the perfection and validity of the King's ideas—Merlyn furiously shouts him down in a memorable speech in which Arthur, while not directly compared to Hitler, is certainly seated at the same table with him:

"Very interesting," he said in a trembling voice. "Very interesting. There was just such a man when I was young—an Austrian who invented a new way of life and convinced himself that he was the chap to make it work. He tried to impose his reformation by the sword, and plunged the civilized world into misery and chaos. But the thing which this fellow had overlooked, my friend, was that he had had a predecessor in the reformation business, called Jesus Christ. Perhaps we may assume that Jesus knew as much as the Austrian did about saving people. But the odd thing is that Jesus did not turn the disciples into storm troopers, burn down the Temple of Jerusalem, and fix the blame on Pontius Pilate. On the contrary, he made it clear that the business of the philosopher was to make ideas *available*, and *not* to impose them on people." (274)

Few men, Arthur included, have been willing to be philosophers alone.

Despite Arthur's weak reasoning about war, he *is* able to remove the element of sport from it and to demonstrate to the nobility who oppose him the bitterness and tragedy heretofore known only to the commoners. He drops all the "etiquette" of warfare by attacking Lot at night, refusing to inflict casualties upon the screen of kerns and dealing only with the perpetrating nobles themselves. He thoroughly defeats Lot and hopes by doing so that all potential opponents will shirk from doing battle with a king who "seemed to accept the death of gentlemen as a part of warfare" (311). For a time, this threat works.

While war is the central topic of discussion in this novel, there is something deeper involved when the Might-harnessed-for-Right theory, surely a noble thought, is so quickly scorned by both Merlyn and White. The simple (and correct) reason for scorning it, I suppose, is the realization that man's free will to make the correct choice in a crucial situation is too often strapped by his own selfishness or, quite often, by uncontrollable circumstance. Arthur, who is certainly a better man than most and who is more able to harness Might than his contemporaries, is spun into the webs of both selfishness and fate by the spiderish Morgause. (In the later novels, of course, he will be by Lancelot and Guenever.) The reason Arthur succumbs to Morgause's seduction can be attributed to a selfish standpoint, to his active libido; but an element of dark fate against which Arthur is relatively helpless is also involved.

As we mentioned earlier, Morgause was initially a re-creation of White's mother, though the bitterest aspects of the characterization were deleted in the revision that Collins demanded.

Nevertheless, similarities are still very close. White once referred to his mother as a "strong-willed, imaginative, selfish, beautiful, malingering" woman who drove her husband to drink and her son to love her passionately until he was eighteen and to despise her thereafter.[13] Morgause has all of these qualities, though her husband is driven to war, not to drink. Perhaps Constance White's most distasteful quality for her son is the same one he emphasizes in Morgause—both were women "for whom all love had to be dependent" and for whom love had to be extracted from "slavish minds."[14] Just as Constance White regarded her son only as something which needed her and whose love she needed (with the return of none from herself), so Morgause seldom sits with her four sons and regards their capture of the unicorn for her as meaningless except as a welcome reassurance that she still has her impersonal hold on their affections.

As the original title of the novel indicates, Morgause is a witch, though "not a serious witch like her sister Morgan Le Fay" (221). This lack of seriousness is a condemnation, not praise; for our first view of the Queen is one in which she is killing a cat in the hope of finding the one bone in its body which, boiled and then sucked upon, would make a person invisible. The cat, a longtime and loving pet, trusts her even until the moment when it is helplessly thrown into a boiling cauldron and cooked alive. The water is so hot that the cat's body falls apart. Morgause gropes for bones and sucks each one while watching herself in the mirror for the moment when her body becomes invisible. After trying several bones without success, she becomes bored and abandons the project. This scene, second to her sons' killing of the unicorn, is the most gruesome one in the novel. The point about Morgause (as about White's mother), however, is clear—things exist in the universe to love her and for her to destroy. Her sons exist for this reason and so does Arthur. She becomes, for White, the symbol of uncontrollable, ideal-wrecking fate.

Having convinced herself that "asses do not mate with pythons" (280)—that she will be unable to seduce English knights (essentially, again, to have them love her and to destroy them)—she decides upon greater targets for "her charms and talents":

> She had been told about Arthur since the army returned—about his strength, charm, innocence and generosity. His splendour had been obvious, even through the envy and suspicion of those he had conquered. Also there had been talk about a girl called Lionore, the daughter of the Earl of Sanam, with whom the young man was supposed to be having an affair. The Queen opened the coffer in the darkness and stood near the moonlit patch from the window, holding a strip of something in her hands. It was like a tape. (316)

The strip is of human skin, called a Spancel, which, when placed over the head of a sleeping man and tied in a bow, gave him two rather distasteful alternatives: if he awakened, he would be dead within a year; if he did not, he would fall in love with the person who had entwined him. Finding Arthur asleep after the great feast of Pellinore's wedding, she is in the act of tying the bow when the King awakens. True to the image of Constance White, the queen obviously would have preferred being loved; but, unable to achieve this end, she will at least destroy what will not love her—or will within a year. Though Arthur lives for many more years, "the Queen of Air and Darkness had a baby by her half-brother nine months later. It was called Mordred" (322–23).

While Arthur is primarily a victim of his own weakness in these events, the element of fate is tremendously important. Much like Oedipus, Arthur does not know who his mother was—Merlyn forgot to tell him. Although Arthur does not marry his mother and kill his father, he is guilty nonetheless of the sin of incest; and the child he begets upon Morgause will be the death of his father and the ruination of his kingdom. Arthur's one moment of weakness, like Oedipus's hotheadedness at the crossroads, negates every noble ideal or heroic action for the rest of his life. For this reason, Morgause, whom we see little of in the book, forms the framing principle by her memorable appearances in the first and last chapters—for, from the time Arthur's war with the Gaelic Confederation first begins, no act of his has any meaning unless it is gauged against the tremendous will of Morgause to fashion an egocentric universe.

Nor is this fate all that Morgause is able to hurl against Arthur's ideals. Her treatment (or mistreatment) of her four sons makes them persons who will all, in one way or another, take out their frustrations upon Arthur and Camelot. In the opening chapter, while their mother cooks the cat below them, the boys recount the story of the ruin of Igraine, the only story their mother has ever told them; and it engenders with each telling more hatred in them for the man they call MacPendragon. For Gareth, the youngest, the tale is one of a "weak and innocent people victimized by a resistless tyranny" (221). Gawaine, the eldest, is "angry because it had been against *his* family" (222). Agravaine, whose life and attitudes toward his mother White seems to be modeling upon his own, "was moved because it was a matter which concerned his mother" about whom "he had curious feelings . . . which he kept to himself" (222). And as for Gaheris, "he did and felt what the others did" (222).

Morgause has been ultimately successful in training the young boys to love her devotedly despite her failure to return their affection; she has also been quite able to pass on to them her ability to destroy anything which suits her purpose. This destructive capability is evident in the ghastly death of the unicorn ––a beautiful, loving, almost sacred animal–which the boys mutilate in their efforts to please Morgause. They *use* the servant girl Meg to lure it; and, as the reluctant girl falls in love with the sweet creature, they carve it up in front of her. The reaction of each to his deed is congruent with the reaction of each to his lineage: Gareth, saddened, wishes he were dead; Gawaine is overcome by a feeling of accomplishment and honor; Agravaine feels vengeful in that, having all the time pretended that Meg was his mother, he has eliminated all that which seems to be getting his share of her love; Gaheris does and feels what the others do.

Each of these young men, trained in his special way to serve as his mother's agent decades later, increases the degree to which uncontrollable fate takes hold of Camelot. As men, these four will not realize they are against Arthur at all; and, fittingly, each is present when Morgause places the Spancel upon Arthur. "The four wild-eyed children from the north were standing behind their mother, shy and defiant, as she was folding the tape" (322).[15] In short, *The Queen of Air and Darkness* forms for the tragedy of Arthur what the legend of the house of Thebes does for the tragedy of Oedipus—a set of inescapable circumstances, ones more fashioned by fate than by human error, which will doom the hero no matter how hard he tries to escape them. Both Merlyn and Tieresias know about this inevitability, but both are impotent to reverse what is preordained. Merlyn's parable about Death in Chapter 10 underscores the great amount of Fate to which even the greatest men are totally subjugated.

Arthur's impending ruin is obviously White's central concern in his second novel; but, like *The Sword in the Stone,* he continues to mock playfully the chivalrous inconsistencies he finds throughout Malory. Having tapped the possibilities of the Questing Beast in the first book, he uses them even more in the second one. White's first thought on the subject seems to have been to wonder why the Questing Beast is not more properly called the Quested Beast. There seems to be some active agency ingrained in the very name, does there not? So, sure enough, when Pellinore, Grummore, and Palomides first sail into this novel on the Magic Barge, Pellinore has lost interest in the chase, for he has fallen in love with the Queen of Flanders' daughter. It is at the outset of this romance that the beast, a female, turns Questing. Noticing that her lifelong entertainment has taken up another pursuit and knowing that knights are forbidden to disregard a challenge, the Beast appears in the woods in the middle of Pellinore's wooing and leads the whole party, the girl excluded, out to sea. Pellinore grows progressively more bored as the Beast grows progressively more elusive. Upon his arrival at Dunlothian, he tells Morgause that he is just plain lovesick.

What follows is White's own peculiar brand of slapstick. Pellinore again abandons the quest, this time to dwell upon thoughts of his beloved Piggy. Grummore and Palomides are equally bored—nothing is happening, for they haven't seen the Beast themselves for days and the whole expedition is flagging. To get things moving again, they ingeniously design a Questing Beast outfit in which they plan to show themselves to Pellinore and thus arouse his interest. Palomides becomes the head and forelegs; Grummore, the other end. After much confusion about getting into the suit and working in unison on the night of the ruse, they set out to meet Pellinore in the suggested spot. Pellinore, questing only to keep his two friends happy, finds nothing; for the fake Beast is late in arriving. Just as the activities are about to start, it begins to rain; Palomides and Grummore are soaked in their skin; and Pellinore, finding that his armor is rusting, goes home. But the fake Beast is unable to retire; for the real Beast, pining for Pellinore in the forest, thinks it has discovered a mate, corners it, and makes advances.

Events complicate themselves even more, for Piggy, Pellinore's lost girl friend, has followed the Beast from Flanders in order to catch up with her beau. Pellinore is elated and, before going off with her, sees what his friends have done. He holds the Beast's tail while the two components of the fake beast run for their lives. The Beast, seeing that Pellinore cares nothing for her and that her other possibility has escaped, begins to cry. Later, however, she becomes more positive and believing her mate to be there, besieges Morgause's castle. The book ends with the Beast's following Palomides to Pellinore's wedding and keeping a sharp eye out lest Palomides prove fickle also.

In many ways these scenes, funny as they are, endanger the unity of the novel. But they also serve in some instances to heighten the real tragedy of Arthur—a tragedy White himself thought too often obscured by the less credible claptrap in the Arthurian tradition. Here, we get the impression that figures like Pellinore and his friends do what they do more because they suspect what posterity will want them to do rather than because they are living their lives the way they would like. Not only do such things as the Questing Beast appear ridiculous by comparison with the struggles of Arthur, but they also seem silly when opposed to such a simple thing as a happy marriage—Pellinore, sick of the chase, wants to do what more normal people do.

The Round Table is a less elaborate case in point. To have such a table which seats one hundred fifty knights would require a table fifty yards in diameter. Merlin and Arthur think this ridiculous; but again because it seems the right thing to do, and Merlyn-the-reversed *knows* it is, they accept the idea. Such demonstrable inconsistencies are all good fun and the reader enjoys them, but really they are White's way of separating the fruit from the chaff in Malory.

What seems less purposeful is the continual ribbing of Ireland and Catholicism. The material is funny, even to the Irish Catholic; but it does not fit, for it is consistent with neither the subject nor the theme of the novel. The points of satire are relatively the same as those upon which White later bases the entire novel *The Elephant and the Kangaroo* and to some extent his book of reminiscences entitled *The Godstone and the Blackymor*. White's biggest quarrels with his landlords, the McDonaghs, were their superstitious approach to their religion and their confused, irrational thinking about any subject of importance whatsoever. Thus, completely to our surprise, White makes such statements as "the incalculable miasma . . . is the leading feature of the Gaelic brain" (249). A similar epithet is also quite often attached to Morgause herself, much to the artistic degradation of her character. Rather than being the crafty, fateful villain White spends so much time creating her to be, she often degenerates into a bungling idiot, not by her actions but by such ill-placed descriptions as these. When White says similar things about St. Toirdealbhach, they are seldom so ruinous, often they are very comical, but they are always out of place in *this* novel. The holy man, the Irish miasma incarnate, tells witch stories to scare his young listeners to God rather than saints' lives to inspire them thereto. Things are more to the point when White mentions religion in Arthur's and Lot's armies ("Arthur's men were revered about [religion] but King Lot's men were not—for such was the custom in all armies that were about to be defeated. . . . Arthur's men knew they were outnumbered . . . so they thought it best to get shriven. King Lot's men, who also knew the odds, spent the night dancing, drinking, dicing, and telling each other dirty stories" [293]), but such commentary is still out of place amidst the central philosophical debate on the morality of warfare. White is at once debating a serious question and peppering it with moral frivolity—to the detriment, once again, of the thematic point. White, who had just moved to Ireland when he was completing this book, must have inserted these jibes tongue in cheek as his finishing touches. Their casual origin is all too obvious, however —they just do not belong there.

Thus, *The Queen of Air and Darkness* seems a novel which is effective in what it says though it is not particularly artistic in the way it says it. The tragic convergence of Morgause and Arthur would have been tightly structured. The necessity of building Arthur's ideals from scratch once again concurrently but profitably loosened this structure, but it profitably heightens the novel's dramatic tension. The satire on chivalry, knighthood, and Questing Beasts, however, dangerously loosened it even more. To introduce irrelevant and personal satire into the midst of all this—that is, the muted attacks on Irish customs—rendered the whole effort diffuse and almost totally structureless. The finished product seems to be no more than a mere connector between two better novels until we realize that here, in this very strange conglomeration of things, is where the tetralogy's crucial questions are first placed in their ultimate tragic perspective.

III The Ill-Made Knight

The Ill-Made Knight, the third volume of the tetralogy, is a better novel in every way. Still loosely structured, as White's condensation of the entire Arthurian legend must necessarily be, it is a wonderful study of three human beings who are in conflict and in love with one another. More than this, White investigates three human beings who are in conflict with themselves when their developed noble ideals fight furiously to overcome their inbred selfishness and inadequacies. Still more, White questions the compatibility of heavenly perfection and earthly humanity within the same person. To be pure for God, it seems, is to renounce the earth and the things of the earth, people included, even to the extent of being uncharitable or naive. Arthur, in attempting to adhere to the principles of his Church and his kingdom, is forced to allow the love affair between his wife and his best friend to proceed unchecked while he trusts God and fate not to annoy him or stir his natural anger. Lancelot, in his continual sway between ideal and human behavior, alienates and disappoints everyone on either end of the spectrum. Guenever, attached almost solely to the human level of thought and action, can support the objectives of Lancelot and Camelot only by trying to keep them beyond her destructive range. The natural humanity of each is thus impaired, and the society in which these characters live is made vulnerable to treasonous forces.

The noble philosophy of the Round Table is destined to fail just because, it seems, the group is composed of men who are neither human nor godly but who try to be an inconsistent combination of both. White demonstrates this combination in many minor ways, but mainly he does so through the three separate portraits of Lancelot, Guenever, and Arthur (and, to some extent, that of Elaine). In retrospect, despite what legend tells us about the great love triangle of Camelot, surprisingly little interaction occurs among the three in White's novel. Arthur stays away from both Lancelot and Guenever so he cannot see what he knows is happening. Lancelot is generally separated from Guenever, either on a quest or in the exile which she imposes; and Guenever complains continually about loneliness.

Maintaining such a separation is advantageous for White in several ways. First, it allows him to carry out a semiphilosophical study of the three ways of leading life: the totally human; the half-human, or half-superhuman; and the totally superhuman. Second, the major question of the tetralogy, which the author first formulated in the preceding book, underscores every action of every character: Arthur's dream continues to crumble from his own and from others' all-too-human mistakes in situations over which the king has no control. Third, the separation heightens the effect of the total inadequacy of Arthur's dream in the first place—Arthur continually adjusts his philosophy to compensate for obvious lacks, which consistently manifest themselves, but he never adjusts it to recognize the inherent inability of most men to place self in a subordinate position to belief. This inability—which we may call the Evil Principle, the devil, or Original Sin—Arthur prefers to ignore because, I suppose, it is staggering to contemplate coping with it.

White's Lancelot is the central figure in the book, for he is the character who realizes all too clearly the presence within himself of this powerful negative force. Even on the first page of the novel White tells us that Lancelot, at this time a boy in his middle teens, has always felt there was "something wrong with him" (327).[16] Initially, the statement seems to have great congruence with his ugly countenance, a face seemingly so ugly that he continually contemplates its reflection in a kettle hat. But White's insistent emphasis upon his face leads us to believe that it has greater significance than merely making Lancelot more realistic than Malory does. When contrasted with his noble deeds, his noble emotions, and his strange appeal to women, the face seems symbolic of an inconsistency or an incongruity in his character (and by extension in the human race). Lancelot, who is not the man to be driven mad by the recognition of a less-than-handsome appearance, has, we are told, a "tendency to madness" (522). During one period in the book (and in the legend), he is insane for two full years. Lancelot seems in the long run a man who, despite his tremendously sincere effort to be pure, is either haunted or, at times, overwhelmed by man's incapacity to be so. While the tetralogy is the story of the tragic ruin of Arthur, *The Ill-Made Knight,* a significant title in many ways, is the recounting of the more cathartic destruction of Lancelot.

White makes every effort to build in Lancelot a character with whom the reader can identify (as he certainly is not in Malory): he is ugly; he will be "the best knight in the world" not because of superhuman birth but because of years of tediously hard work in which he is often bruised, scarred, and discouraged; and his initial love for Arthur is that of a Bronx boy for Mickey Mantle—he is a hero-worshiper. When, after having met the king some years earlier, Lancelot discovers that Arthur no longer remembers his name, he is crushed and sulks for days. He has a guardian, Uncle Dap, who he feels consistently stifles his enthusiasm with demonstrations of life's hard realities. Even as Lancelot develops as a knight under Dap's tutelage, he never loses the sense of insecurity he has felt from his earliest memories. He is shown, all in all, to be a young man who, with a severe rearing behind him, sets out in the world, as do all young men, not really knowing whether or not the world will accept him.

But, despite his insecurity his goals are evident; but these, too,

White places in more realistic perspective than does Malory. Early in the novel Lancelot has a dream which White summarizes in this way:

> Lancelot and his young brother, Ector Demaris, had been sitting in two chairs. They got out of these chairs and were mounted on two horses. Lancelot said: "Go we, and seek that which we shall not find." So they did. But a Man or a Power set upon Lancelot, and beat him and despoiled him, and clothed him in another array which was full of knots, and made him ride on an ass instead of on the horse. Then there was a beautiful well, with the fairest waters he had ever seen, and he got off his ass to drink out of it. It seemed to him that there could be nothing in the world more beautiful than to drink of this well. But as soon as he stooped his lips toward it, the water sank away. It went right down into the barrel of the well, sinking and sinking from him so that he could not get it. It made him feel desolate, to be abandoned by the water of the well. (329)

While the dream is contrapuntal to various incidents later in the book (Galahad's demeaning of him is one), it is, I think, more metaphysically relevant to Lancelot as a member of mankind. Even at this early age he will not deceive himself by assuming that all he seeks, or even the greater part of it, will be found. Yet his goals remain, though tempered, high. His love for Arthur makes him want to be the best knight in the world, though he never expects to achieve his ambition. His love for God and his religion leads him to "want to be able to perform some ordinary miracle—to head a blind man or something like that, for instance" (335). To the medieval mind, such an ability was taken as a sign from God that his life was being led correctly. The presence of the word "ordinary" is some indication, I think, of Lancelot's estimation of his own ability to do anything which would impress God.

With these ideals and these fears, Lancelot gamely sets out for Camelot. A "love-triangle" has necessarily already developed, but on the surface it is not so impossibly incompatible as the term itself ordinarily implies. The medieval theory of love, a theory White, Arthur, and Lancelot all seem to recognize, centers itself around the Neoplatonic theory of *Agape* and the Augustinian concept of *caritas.* Oversimplified, both terms mean "proper loving," which, to a medieval man, meant to do everything, no matter how mundane or undignified, for the love of God.[17] To do anything for earthly ends alone—write a book, love a woman, fight a duel, anything at all—was to be guilty of the grave sin of *cupiditas*. In short, God must be constantly in mind. Chaucer, especially in *The Canterbury Tales,* demonstrates that the eye of the needle becomes even narrower with such a theory—it is extremely difficult to think constantly of an abstract idea—and Chaucer's Parson and Plowman seem the only ones capable of such concentration. Thus, in Lancelot's triangle—one which includes himself, Arthur, and God—the potential for *caritas* is present. To interpret Arthur's dream in spiritual terms and to pursue it and defend it with integrity is to possess *caritas.* When the triangle becomes a quadrangle, however, as it does almost immediately with the addition of Guenever, the more easily attainable *cupiditas* necessarily takes control.

Lancelot departs for Camelot at the opening of Chapter 4; by the beginning of the next chapter, he is already tacitly in love with Guenever, and she with him. It is surprising that, within the course of the intervening chapter, Lancelot has both been jealous of, and disliked by, the queen. His jealousy is an initial reaction to Arthur's marriage, for the young man feels that he will never have the king's love to the degree he requires it; but his dislike of her is more telling and more complicated. When Guenever accompanies him on a falconry expedition soon after his arrival, she is unintentionally more of a hindrance than a help. When Lancelot more or less tells her so, he surprises himself by being pleased at the hurt look in her eyes. Shortly thereafter he realizes that, had he not injured her, he might never have fallen in love with her: "He might never have noticed her as a person, if he had not seen the pain in her eyes" (353). Because Lancelot's insecurity in the face of the perfection of Camelot has evidently led him to expect almost angelic men at court, his awareness of the humanity he despises in himself in these people reduces this insecurity considerably. "Hurt" must be defined carefully in Lancelot's case; he is quick to help people in distress and is equally fast at granting mercy to conquered knights—but he has seen the hurt, the humanity, in their eyes; and this quality is all he requires. Later in the book, a more mature and experienced Lancelot finally accuses himself of self-pride in his own behavior. He discovers one thing very early at Camelot: if he cannot be the superior of the knights of the Round Table because of his inbred deficiencies, he is at least their equal.

Guenever can, of course, do nothing positive in terms of Lancelot's search for purity before God (*caritas*). Lancelot cannot really regard Arthur as a man dedicated to the will of God and at the same time fight for Arthur's dream and seduce his wife. Thus, when Lancelot insists that his love for Arthur is undiminished by his relationship with Guenever, something rings false. It is obvious that he still loves Arthur and that he loves Guenever despite her harsh treatment of him. But Lancelot has lost sight of God; or, more properly, he sacrilegiously, though unintentionally, lowers God to the level of a person who is equal but not superior to Arthur and Guenever. Lancelot feels compelled to direct all his actions not toward God but generally toward any one of the three who most need his help. Such a value system, of course, is a rather unlikely, but in Lancelot's case, possible form of *cupiditas.* He often loses sight of the ideals of God and Camelot, and he sees them as equals which charity demands that he treat well. They are ends in themselves—even God is a person and not a deity.

Lancelot is guilty of the sin of *cupiditas* long before his relationship with Guenever becomes a physical one. When he goes forth on his first quest, the one in which he defeats Turquaine and Carados, he is not fighting for the godly ideals which Arthur's court represents, or even for fame and glory as a man of God, but is simply getting away from Guenever lest his sexual desires overcome him. He hides in his religion in order to solve his problems rather than overcome them through positive commitment to the right. This, too, is *cupiditas,* for the quest is not for the glory of God as the primary end. So stern a judgment may seem like quibbling, but Lancelot (and his age) is an expert quibbler. He has a fine sense of right and wrong in terms of his religion; and, in questing for a negative purpose, he knows he is wrong. When he sends all the knights he conquers home to do homage to Guenever and not to God, he all but openly admits his error.

Yet his ability to resist an affair with the queen is meaningful to him despite his ever clearer recognition of the contrary forces within himself. But the second quest on which the weakening Guenever orders him proves to be his undoing and in this episode one of the great ironies of the entire tetralogy occurs. Having journeyed to the kingdom of King Pelles, he is enthuiastically sought by the citizenry for the purpose of rescuing the king's daughter Elaine from the boiling kettle in which Morgan Le Fay had thrown her many years ago. When Lancelot, now assuredly the best knight in the world, accomplishes this heretofore impossible task with ease, he suddenly realizes that God has finally allowed him his long-sought miracle. In the moment of God's greatest love, however, Lancelot forgets to return it; for, as soon as Elaine is released from the pot, Lancelot stations himself to receive the thanks of the town, to which Elaine somewhat playfully but ironically says: "'Ought we go to Church now and thank God as well as you?'" (387). Lancelot compensates for his oversight gracefully, but the tone of what is about to happen is evident.

On the surface, Lancelot is seemingly not guilty when he loses his purity to Elaine several days later. Still pure-hearted, the knight fails to realize the girl is falling in love with him. But mere amorous advances in themselves are not nearly enough to victimize a knight as strong as he; thus, when the moment arrives for Elaine and her butler to drug Lancelot, he does not respond to the seductions of Elaine or to the drug but to the fabricated story that Guenever, without Arthur, is staying at a castle not five miles away. Thus, while Elaine literally steals Lancelot's purity and his might when she tricks him into sleeping with her, Lancelot is certainly not guiltless—his lust is self-actuated and only the objects of it are switched since he thinks he is sleeping with Guenever. Thereafter, he considers himself to be a miserable living lie; and he sees no reason, having deprived himself of God, to deny himself Guenever.

Though White sincerely tried to avoid a second villainess in his tetralogy (Morgause was effective enough), Guenever is treated rather roughly. She has none of the noble ideals of either her husband or Lancelot. She is not evil, however; she simply fares poorly in comparison. Her initial (and perhaps her ultimate) problem is immaturity; for, though she is Lancelot's age, she has never subjected her body or soul to the youthful rigors he has. She is much younger than Arthur; and, while she loves him, she sees little of him and is, as any young girl would be, overwhelmed by the presence of such knightly talent on all sides. When she falls in love with the new knight Lancelot, she twice orders him to undertake lengthy quests from unclear motivations. Her religion is not strong enough, and she seems to understand little of what her husband's philosophy comprises; indeed, her guiding principle seems more a simple recognition of the historical dislike of adulterous queens and a resolve not to have history anathematize her. Guenever is neither strong enough either to have Lancelot at Camelot or to have him absent. Her love and her loneliness grow steadily; and, when her lover returns from the quest on which he lost his purity and his integrity and when Arthur thereupon announces that he will be away from Camelot for two years, neither the pining queen nor the dejected knight is strong enough to resist the other any longer.

Perhaps Guenever's most predominant vice is selfishness. Linked with Lancelot's lingering idealism, this combination causes their years together to be almost intolerably complicated. He is continually torn between his love for her and the loss of his long-developed power to do great things. When he reveals to her that his happiness is stifled by "sin," she selfishly chides him for ruining their relationship with silly fears. When he states what the "sin" specifically is, she is furious that he has indulged in an adulterous love with anyone but her. On the surface, Guenever's jealousy seemingly drives Lancelot into two years of insanity; but, as far as White's version of the legend is concerned, this reading is a superficial one. Lancelot has spent his entire life preparing to be the best knight in the world, and he seemed for a time well on his way. But progressively darker shades of *cupiditas* began to loom over his ideals: he fell in love with Guenever and out of love with God, he quested for purposes of escape alone, he lost his purity to one woman while thinking he was losing it to another—and, with nothing of his original strength remaining, he cannot even find a mundane, fleshly sort of happiness with the immature, temperamental, intolerant queen. Something evil within him, something for which he is willing to accept total blame has wrecked every yearning of his short life.

During the two years that follow his break with Guenever, he serves as a fool in the court of Pelles though he is a worldly wise fool of a Shakespearean play, to be sure. When he finally regains his senses and his identity is discovered, Lancelot seems resolved not to seek impossible dreams. He decides to return to Elaine, the mother of his illegitimate son; but he will not do so because of love but because of a sense of duty and a feeling of pity; he is ready to sacrifice his life for the happiness of two other people to whom he has a substantial measure of responsibility. Resigned to be a human being, he no longer aspires to be the superman he had always envisioned himself. Supermen are vulnerable to the destructive forces of evil and are easily undone.

Like Arthur, however, Lancelot has been bred for and trained for idealistic quests—quests after human and social perfection—and Lancelot cannot long be satisfied with the ordinary domesticity offered by Elaine. When two knights of the Round Table come in search of him, he fights furiously his desires to return; but, when Uncle Dap arrives with his armor, his higher instincts finally win; and he leaves the stoic Elaine who must now wait twenty years for his return. White, perhaps significantly, says little about Lancelot's first fifteen years at Camelot; for Lancelot is obviously enduring a period of retraining. Upon his departure from Elaine, his ideals are confused, as is the case with those of all the knights of the Round Table who have also discovered that the ideal life is nigh impossible. Lancelot's retraining is not, therefore, the same as the training he had endured as a youth; for what Arthur and his men now represent is something entirely different.

We have to this point ignored Arthur in this novel; but Arthur is still the central figure of the tetralogy and still, for all his faults, its most notable character. In *The Sword in the Stone*, we saw Arthur the enthusiastic student of the world as it is. In *The Queen of Air and Darkness*, we saw Arthur the architect of the world as it ought to be. In *The Ill-Made Knight*, we see Arthur an older and wiser idealist who is beginning to notice that imposing ideals on the world is like fighting a hydra; but, even at the conclusion of this novel, he still seems to feel that the only thing to do is keep fighting and perhaps eventually the heads will suddenly stop multiplying and finally disappear. Arthur's problem is even more difficult than Lancelot's because Arthur must fight Lancelot's battle several hundred times; for Lancelot is to Arthur as a microcosm is to a macrocosm. Lancelot fights a furious battle to overcome only his own instincts, whereas Arthur must overcome, as well as his own, those of every knight at his table and of many who are not. Ideals are pursuable only as long as self-interest can be held in abeyance. As Lancelot has proved, to hold one self aside is an enormous task; to hold several hundred aside is impossible.

And so, while *The Queen of Air and Darkness* demonstrates Arthur's inability to maintain total control of himself, *The Ill-Made Knight* shows Arthur's ever-decreasing power over those around him. Even at the outset, when he is first knocked off his horse by Lancelot, we have a sign of things to come. We know even now that Gawaine has killed a lady and that Pellinore has committed a foolish act, killed the King of Orkney, which will eventually stir grave trouble in the kingdom. Bringing home the man he is sure will be his best knight, Arthur quickly sees this man stealing his wife. In his observations of the developing relationship between his wife and Lancelot, Arthur is shown to have a serious character flaw, one which is bound to be that of every man who attempts to live perfectly in an imperfect world:

> Arthur's feelings completed the misery of the court. He, unfortunately for himself, had been beautifully brought up. His teacher had educated him as the child is educated in the womb, where it lives the history of man from fish to mammal—and, like the child in the womb, he had been protected with love meanwhile. The effect of such an education was that he had grown up without any of the useful accomplishments for living—without malice, vanity, suspicion, cruelty, and the commoner forms of selfishness. Jealousy seemed to him the most ignoble of vices. He was sadly unfitted for hating his best friend or for torturing his wife. He had been given too much love and trust to be good at these things. (406)

Arthur's solution, as a result, is to ignore the problem—ignore the very humanity which causes such problems—and to hope that fate will not take action against it. Such handling of this problem is really just another statement of the basic weakness in Arthur's dream: material beings are not easily convinced to do only purely spiritual things. By ignoring the materiality of his court, Arthur ignores the internal disease which must eventually emaciate the beautiful externals of what he is attempting to create.

We do not imply that Arthur does not really see the power of human nature; we suggest only that his solutions to the problem are repeatedly superhuman and, thus, superficial. For instance, early in this novel Arthur is pointedly aware that his efforts, like those of many modern powers, to bring peace to the world are drenching it in a bloodbath from which it might not survive. This result is due in great part, he feels, to the competitive instinct which he, himself, has instilled in his knights. This realization seems to bring with it a tacit admission of the sin of *cupiditas*; for Arthur, by his own admission, has never placed the concept of God close enough to the center of his and his knights' endeavors. They have been trying to bring Right to the world, but they seem to be doing so for their own greater honor and glory. When Might for Right is achieved in Arthur's middle age, the misdirected knights continue to fight one another—an extension of their true purposes in the first place; and Arthur resolves to redirect the efforts of the Round Table:

> "I thought we could start by trying to achieve something which would be helpful to the spirit, if you see what I mean. We have achieved the bodily things: peace and prosperity: now we lack work. If we invent another bodily employment, a temporal employment—mere empire building or something like that—we shall be faced by the same problem again, probably worse, as soon as it has been achieved. But why can't we pull our Table together by turning its energies to the spirit? You know what I mean by the spirit. If our Might was given a channel so that it worked for God, instead of for the rights of man, surely that would stop the rot, and be worth doing?" (456–57)

This redirection of Arthur's is White's version of the initiation of the Grail quest, but White keeps the quests for the Holy Grail at a distance from the reader. He devotes three chapters to the Grail finders themselves—Galahad, Bors, and Percival—but their exploits are related by the three unsuccessful knights who return. In each of their tales variations of the central themes of the tetralogy are debated. First Gawaine tells of Galahad's cocky behavior and of how he, when given the choice between the selfish and the mannerly, always does the selfish thing. This choice seems incongruous until the reformed Lancelot later points out that one so perfectly pure as Galahad has an obligation to follow his own instincts rather than the preformed rules of worldly chivalry which, as has been continually seen, gratify the individual ego. Gawaine, disgusted that Galahad has been allowed fulfillment in the quest, fails even to realize that the typical chivalrous approach is not fit for godly things. In contrast to Gawaine, Galahad defies a system which badly needs reforming.

Sir Lionel relates the tale of Sir Bors, a man so pure that he will not seduce a woman in order to save twelve lives. This display horrifies Lionel, and the tale stuns the very pragmatic Guenever who comments upon Bors's inhumanity. Bors is obviously one of the few Round Table knights on the quest who understands that the will of God is more important than the individual or collective wills of men. Finally, Sir Aglovale tells the story of Percival; and Aglovale seems the only one of the three narrators who learns anything from the subject of his narrative. Percival on the quest is outstanding for his perfect simplicity and innocence—for his adherence to the childlike state which Christ said gets man into heaven. From his example, Aglovale, tremendously overcome at the news of the death of his father, Pellinore, learns forgiveness and patience—much to the relief and satisfaction of Arthur.

But for every Aglovale there are fifty who have vented their "Games-Mania" on a spiritual quest in the same way they had on secular ones. Half have been killed, and a few who had gained any degree of perfection at all have chosen not to return. Again Arthur's solutions to the problems of his shaky table have failed, thereby leaving his Utopia less Utopian than before since the worst of the knights remain. The clothes of the knights are ridiculously elaborate, "marital fidelity had become 'news'" (504), and scandal is the subject of the day. Rumor and suspicion inbreed to the point of entangling his wife when she seems to be the likely suspect as the murderer of Sir Patrick. Yet Arthur still ignores the fact that human nature will never respond collectively to abstract ideals. By the end of the novel, Might is Right has been changed by Arthur to Might for Right, which failed; to Might for the Spirit, which failed; to abstract Justice without Might, which will fail; to Law as Might, which usually works—but that seems to be where everything started in the first place. But Law as Might is the subject of *The Candle in the Wind.*

While the Grail Quest has failed as far as Arthur is concerned, Lancelot's reaction is distinctly different. Even though he fails badly in his attempt, Lancelot returns a new man. First, of all, his son Galahad has found the Grail and unhorsed his father in the process. Lancelot, having reconciled himself for years to the fact that he will never be the world's greatest knight, is gratified to see his son be the chief contender for the role he had vacated before ever attaining it. More than this, however, Galahad has demonstrated that the rewards of purity are worth striving for; and Lancelot becomes severely penitent, but positively so. When he returns to Camelot in a hair shirt, he naturally desires to confess to Arthur about his affairs with the Queen. The unredeemed and aging Guenever, of course, prevents this. But the important thing is that Lancelot is now fully aware of his pride—his *cupiditas* in doing everything for himself, his desire to have power over life and death in every encounter.

Galahad has sought and found God, the theological ideal; but Lancelot has, for most of his life, sought and lost God as a displaceable equal—as a man who just happened somehow to be chosen to be God and who could not hold the position in the face of the best knight in the world. Lancelot, of course, never formulates this view and, in fact, never realizes it until he reflects upon his failure while on the Grail quest. Three humiliating defeats on the quest itself convince him that God is a fantastically powerful Being who is in complete control of, and therefore unimpressed by, the petty accomplishments of mortals. In these three defeats, God withheld "the special gift of victory" (491) which Lancelot had always before taken for granted; and, by doing so, God demonstrates to Lancelot's receptive spirit the long but worthwhile path to spiritual perfection.

We know, however, that this resolve, at least in the legend, is not Lancelot's ultimate one. Through the remainder of this novel and throughout *The Candle in the Wind,* he continues to vacillate between his love of God and of Guenever. Yet, White, Arthur, and perhaps God seem to realize the struggle with which he is faced; and they honor the sincere attempt he is making to survive it morally. This appreciation seems to be evident in the concluding scene of *The Ill-Made Knight* in which Lancelot, by the power of his faith and ideals alone, closes the wound and saves the life of Sir Urre. Lancelot has been allowed by God and by Arthur the miracle he has always sought but has never hoped to attain. In the last paragraph of the novel, he is kneeling in prayer amidst a throng of jubilant knights and ladies. His troubles continue in the ensuing volume; but, when all is considered in retrospect, this moment is the zenith of Lancelot's life.

Though I still feel that *The Ill-Made Knight* is not quite the achievement that *The Sword in The Stone* is, it certainly represents White's finest attempt at complex characterization. Its three main characters never dwindle, as too many White creations do, to the simplistic—they are torn and wracked people throughout, but they never lose the will to continue their pursuit of elusive Truth and perfection. A compelling book, this novel is the core of the tetralogy in terms of thematic unity and development. The tradition White humor, satire, and lightness of touch are missing in it—yet the novel succeeds tremendously well.

IV The Candle in the Wind

The Candle in the Wind,[18] the last book in the Arthurian tetralogy, forms a powerful and emotional climax to White's masterpiece. Though technically flawed in several obvious ways, the raw cathartic scenes which take place among Arthur, Lancelot, Mordred, and Gawaine, and especially the penultimate one between the doomed King and the young page whom he orders to carry his plan into the future, survive the defects themselves by greatly obscuring them. The major flaw in the book stems from the fact that it is nearly all dialogue carried out in prearranged scenes among carefully selected and carefully moving groups of characters. In changing it from its original form as drama to novel, White seems to have done little more than remove the stage directions and convert a few long speeches from spoken lines to narrative passages. Thus, the plot and setting, which swept so broadly across all of Europe in the first three books, are now limited to rooms in castles and battlefield tents. The book's biggest and most spectacular scene—the one in which Lancelot rescues Guenever from the stake and accidentally kills Gareth and Gaheris in the process—is related only through the perfunctory words of Arthur and Gawaine, who watch him with mixed emotions from a castle window.

The fourth novel, of course, would be the least likely to be severely hurt by the mixture of dramatic and novelistic techniques. The themes are long since clear, and the character relationships and conflicts have complicated themselves to a tremendous degree. Not much more than introspection and resolution should be happening in the last book of the tetralogy and reflective tranquility is more conducive to its needs than the fierce action of the earlier books. Moreover, the absence of physical action in this book allows the character of Mordred to dominate the situation, a domination which is essential if the collapse of Arthur's dream is to make thematic sense.

Mordred functions in this last part as both a character and a symbol. The illegitimate son of Arthur by Morgause (who is also the mother of Agravaine, Gawaine, Gaheris, and Gareth), Mordred appears as the wronged child who is vitriolic and revengeful because of what has happened to him and because of the harm Arthur seems to have done to the morals of his curious mother. The tone is established in the very first chapter when Mordred manipulates Agravaine's weak will to achieve the destruction of Arthur and his kingdom. Though his brother warns Mordred that their cause would lack popular support and that alone they would be unable to overcome the allegiance of Arthur and Lancelot, Mordred insists that revelation of the affair between Lancelot and Arthur's wife will not only gain public support but cause weakness within the ranks of the opposition. Agravaine, of course, is easily convinced of both the possibility and the profit of such a plan; but Gawaine, Gaheris, and Gareth refuse to willingly take part in it. These three brothers are still idealistically attached to Arthur's dream and are also physically indebted to the courage and purity of Sir Lancelot.

Just before Mordred and Agravaine confront Arthur with their dictum, Gawaine summarizes the tragedy of their wills: " 'It is a trouble . . . that will aye destroy the flower of chivalry in all the world: a mischief to our noble fellowship: and all by the cause of two unhappy knights' " (586).[19]

As a character, Mordred is, then, the physical enemy of "the flower of chivalry," but as a symbol he is more universally and tragically horrifying. Always dressed in black, Mordred is the symbol of the complexity of evil which denies the abilities of even the most noble individuals to perfect themselves. There are two major types of evil represented in this one man. The first is that which man creates himself—the skeleton in the closet, to put it tritely. As a young man, Arthur had indulged in illicit sexual relations with a woman whom he had found intriguing; had created an unwanted child; and then, with the passion of a nineteen-year-old, had attempted to drown the son and several other innocent children by placing them in a boat and leaving it to wreck itself on the coastal rocks. Mordred, who accidentally survived, now forever stands against what Arthur tries to construct at Camelot. Mordred's survival is an omen to Arthur: " ' . . . God saved Mordred, and sent him back to shame me afterwards' " (579). Since Mordred is responsible for Arthur's death, the destruction of the Round Table, and the relegation of Guenever and Lancelot to a religious life, Camelot and its ideals seem to have been destroyed by a flaw within itself and its founder.

Yet, while Arthur's culpability cannot be denied, it can be somewhat restricted; for, on a second level, Mordred represents an evil which is metaphysical as well as personal. In *The Queen of Air and Darkness* Morgause, Arthur's seducer, is clearly described as a universal force which has as its main function the ensnarement of human beings. Morgause, the active participant in Arthur's loss of virginity and in the eventual production of the evil Mordred, is the Queen of Air and Darkness, the Witch in the Wood. She is an outside force which will not allow pure and noble instincts. Most men corrupt themselves with little urging; Arthur required urging, and the universe provided him with it. This dual significance of Mordred is exactly what makes the resolution of this novel so difficult for Arthur the character,

White the writer, and us the readers. The ultimate question to be asked is whether Arthur ever had a chance for success in the first place—from the very day he took the sword from the anvil.

To gain any kind of answer to this question, we must notice several things about Arthur himself. As an active and purposeful character, he does survive beyond the middle of the third book; for, when he began to realize that human nature—though it might be, as Merlyn had said, highly perfectible—was not to be perfected easily, his inclination was to look the other way when things began to go wrong. His great love for Lancelot and his intense desire to protect order and tranquility in his kingdom cause him to permit an illicit love affair to go unchallenged. The young and idealistic Arthur had stepped forthrightly into the universe to destroy what was evil within it, but he now begins to compromise. In the fourth book, the first three times we see Arthur he accidentally walks into treasonous and sinful situations; but he pretends not to know what is going on. The first time he does so, he arrives directly in the middle of a fist fight among the five Orkney brothers about the question of destroying the chivalric basis of the kingdom; but Arthur "does not notice"—he wants no trouble. In the next scene, when he accidentally opens the door upon a flirtation session between Lancelot and Guenever, the king retreats and seeks a page to announce him. In still the next scene, Arthur tries to talk Mordred and Agravaine out of their complaints even before they have expressed them.

The point, of course, is that Arthur cannot conquer evil by pretending that it no longer exists. Thus, the contrast between the evil Mordred and the virtuous Arthur resembles that between the willful Ahab and the shrinking Starbuck; and both the *Pequod* and Camelot are destroyed because the virtuous man was the weaker one. Though Arthur debates the improbability of perfection at great lengths in his tent in the final chapter, the fact that he seeks a boy to carry his message into the future seems to indicate that neither it nor the theme is one of fatalism and consequent resignation.

Lancelot, on the other hand, in total consistency with his development toward the end of *The Ill-Made Knight*, still seems to feel that active vice and active virtue can coexist like hot and cold water in the same tap. He fights Arthur's battles by day; fornicates with Arthur's wife by night; and, now late in life, seems to prefer love to fighting. Yet Lancelot, who still has a sense of right conscience that will not desert him, does not like his two-faced behavior and wishes Guenever would leave with him for France so that they might again live honestly and openly. The love for Arthur's wife he cannot repress, but the false image he can. This more-than-bravado-or-rashness (Lancelot is far too old to resort to either) explains his bold decision to visit the Queen's chamber despite the warning from Gareth that Mordred is preparing to trap and expose him as her illicit lover. When, in fact, he *is* cornered in her bedroom, he and Guenever immediately decide that he should escape and then return openly to rescue her from the hands of the state, for even the pragmatic Queen now realizes that their sin is a public one. Her devotion to Arthur had hitherto been the expression of a desire to protect her position with Lancelot and not to embarrass the king before his kingdom. Now, since neither can be prevented, she resolves to leave as soon as Lancelot can so arrange it.

The public shame of his wife and best friend places Arthur in a tremendously difficult position. Heretofore assaulted with the problem of evil, he is now confronted with the problem of justice. Whereas he could afford to ignore (it seemed) evil, he cannot disregard either that which has been publicly made known or that sense of order which the spirit of Camelot demands. He had clandestinely warned the lovers that misconduct, if detected, would have to be severely punished—and now the detection has been made. Torn between his love for his wife and friend and his love for the ideals upon which his kingdom was founded—much as Captain Vere (if we might refer again to Melville) was torn between the purity of Billy Budd and the shaking of a necessary order—Arthur condemns his wife to burn at the stake. He does not feel this judgment to be just, but he does feel it to be necessary. To make the problem more complicated, the accuser is Mordred, who had participated in the murder of his own mother for the same crime as Guenever's. Arthur feels not only that he must be man enough to respond in kind but also that he owes Mordred anything he wishes simply because he is responsible for Mordred's very miserable existence. Mordred's symbolic stature is again clear—instead of divorcing himself from the sin of his past, Arthur continues, as with a bad habit, to become its victim.

Because the justice of law and that of the heart are two different things, Arthur, true to his nature, tries to formulate a plan in which both can coexist. When he plants a loose guard around Guenever's stake, he hopes that Lancelot will sweep her away to France "'...and all the forms of justice will be satisfied'" (618). Yet, on the day of the burning, even this plan, which seemed at first so right, suddenly seems fraught with wrong:

> "What is right?" cried the old man, looking after him with a face of misery. "What is wrong? If Lancelot does come to rescue her, he may kill those innocent fellows of the guard, which I have set to burn her. They have trusted me and I have put them there to keep him off, because it is justice. If he saves her, they will be killed. If they are not killed, she will be burned. But burned to death, Gawaine, in horrible, burning flames—and she is my much-loved Gwen." (611)

Although the scene when Lancelot does arrive is somewhat comic (Gawaine has to ask which side Arthur means when he shouts "'We shall win!'"), the tragic aftermath reveals that Lancelot had mistakenly killed Gareth and Gaheris in the fight (both were unarmed because they feared harming the knight, Lancelot, they so deeply loved). Once again, Arthur's desire to represent the highest standards of Truth in his decisions—to be totally just and to offset all the conflicts the very word Truth implies—has created an even greater evil than before.

In this respect, Gawaine, Arthur's closest companion in this final book of the tetralogy, is an interesting study. Arthur's father, Uther Pendragon, had killed Gawaine's father; Arthur had had illicit relations with Gawaine's mother, because of which Gawaine himself participated in his mother's murder; and his brother Agravaine was killed by Lancelot on the night of the bedroom trap. Gawaine, who is able to see all of these incidents in perspective, always realizes the tremendous conflicts involved in the right and wrong of each incident. The murder of his two younger brothers, Gareth and Gaheris, is, however, too much for him to bear. Although he constantly recalls that Lancelot was responsible for his very survival in several encounters and although he realizes that Lancelot was in the present matter more a victim of circumstances than an intentional murderer, Lancelot suddenly becomes for him the symbol of all the evil and disorder in a life he desperately wanted to be so virtuous and orderly. As a result, Gawaine vows to pursue Lancelot until either he or his new enemy is dead. The very emotions which rule him are the same emotions which, though more intelligently and rationally handled, initially motivated Arthur in his search of the ideals of Camelot.

In catering to the social order once, Arthur must do so a second time as well. The integrity of the kingdom necessitates that he launch an attack on Lancelot, and thus evil is once again unleashed in Camelot while Mordred gleefully watches in the background. Before the attack can be launched, however, Lancelot and Guenever, knowing that war is to be waged, arrange to have a papal bull sent to Arthur which orders all hostilities to cease. They do; Guenever is returned in ignominy to Arthur; and Lancelot is banished forever. After Gawaine informs him that he has fifteen days to leave and that then he will be pusued, Lancelot reluctantly leaves; and the three central figures, who have loved each other so much, will never again be together.

With the head, heart, and soul of Camelot now parted forever, all that remains to happen is total collapse. Arthur, now blind to all right and wrong, leaves Mordred (evil) in charge of his kingdom and goes with Gawaine (the last representative of his dream) to France in pursuit of Lancelot. Arthur, of course, does not want to capture or murder the Frenchman; but he does want to be with Gawaine at the end he sees is sure to come. While Arthur is in France, Mordred declares himself king and forces a promise of marriage from Guenever. By this time, Arthur's bastard son is totally mad; and he envisions a marriage to the Queen as a fitting repayment to his father for the incest of which he himself was born. Meanwhile, in France, Gawaine has been defeated several times by Lancelot but has been released unharmed. Mortified, Gawaine, knowing he cannot forsake his quest, wishes that Lancelot would kill him so the whole distasteful business could end. Gawaine is fighting for a purpose he cannot respect, and Arthur and Lancelot have nothing left for which to fight. Dissolution is nearly complete.

In the tetralogy's last three chapters, a new note of hope and purpose is lightly struck—a note which the reader must strain to hear amidst the clamor of battle and the noise of warring consciences. In Chapter 12, Arthur receives word of Mordred's treason at home, and he and Gawaine hurry their armies across the English Channel to fight something they now are sure is worth combating. In the following chapter, Lancelot hears about what is happening in England; and, because of his continued loyalty to Arthur and his love of Guenever, he moves his army to assist his former friends. In several days of battle both Gawaine and Arthur are killed, as is Mordred. Knowing that the battle is finally won but that they themselves are too corrupted to fight again, Lancelot and Guenever enter a monastery and a convent. As they do so, they leave behind them their triumphs and their failures as examples from which the next generation may learn in order that its crusade against all that is evil and inhumane may be carried forth more cleanly and more decisively than that waged by the knights of the Round Table had been.

But the ending of the novel itself is not nearly so important as the last scenes before the fatal battle, which occur in Arthur's tent near Salisbury on the night before his death. In a series of powerful and compelling monologues, Arthur reflects upon and summarizes his failures and accomplishments, including therein musings upon the history and the future of the human race. In these several pages, all that the tetralogy has been about congeals into a tremendous set of questions, both those which have been answered and those which have not; and these Arthur passes on to the young page, who in turn will pass them, hopefully with a few more answered, to the generations that succeed him.

In a very negative and pessimistic summation of his dream, Arthur seeks the root of its failure. Beginning to make biblical associations which he had hitherto ignored, Arthur determines that, because of original sin, man was basically wicked and deceitful; and, thus, his ideas of "chivalry and justice became a child's illusions . . ." (667). From his first inclination to blame man, Arthur progresses to the next step; he blames the universe for making man the way he is:

Perhaps man was neither good nor bad, was only a machine in an insensate universe—his courage no more than a reflex to danger, like the automatic jump at the pin-prick. Perhaps there were no virtues, unless jumping at pin-pricks was a virtue, and humanity only a mechanical donkey led on by the iron carrot of love, through the pointless treadmill of reproduction. Perhaps Might was a law of Nature, needed to keep the survivors fit. Perhaps he himself. . . . (667)

From his reflection about determinism, he proceeds to place the possible blame upon those men, especially himself, who were ordained by God or the universe to lead men out of the roles of donkeys into those of human perfection and who, instead, led them into more animalism than they had had before. The natural inclination of all the leaders of history had been to avenge wrong with wrong rather than to separate themselves from the past and to begin anew. Thus, instead of giving man a chance for rebirth, the leaders of men had given them warfare. Despite good intentions that the war in which they submerged themselves was to be the last one, somehow, a new war started even before the old war had ended.

Arthur, weary, continues to think. Perhaps, he reflects, the problem has been that the men who had directed such wars had never been capable of separating their "selves" and their desire to gratify these "selves" from the supposedly noble cause for which they were, on the surface, fighting. Possession became, in the long run, the root of every war—those-who-had-not determined, at a given point in time, to take whatever it was away from those-who-had. He reflects upon another passage from the Bible: "God had told people that they would have to cease to live as individuals. They would have to go into the force of life, like a drop falling into a river. God had said that it was only the men who could give up their jealous selves, their futile individualities of happiness and sorrow, who would die peacefully and enter the ring. He that would save his life was asked to lose it" (670–71). Arthur realizes that man is not capable of such abnegation because man questions both the very existence of God and the good will of his fellow man. To his confused and contradictory reasoning, the tired king appends this summation:

Suspicion and fear: possessiveness and greed: resentment for ancestral wrong: all these seemed to be a part of it. Yet they were not the solution. He could not see the real solution. He was too old and tired and miserable to think constructively. He was only a man who had meant well, who had been spurred along that course of thinking by an eccentric necromancer with a weakness for humanity. Justice had been his last attempt—to do nothing which was not just. But it had ended in failure. To do at all had proved too difficult. He was done himself. (671)

Had White's tale ended here, something would obviously have been missing. All the results of Camelot are certainly, in the long run, negative; but the attempt itself, and the ideals which the attempt embodied, must surely be worth more than the philosophical and theological junk pile. What exactly Camelot was worth neither Arthur nor T. H. White ever literally says; but, for the reader, positive possibilities, despite the negative results, glow brightly in the distance. In an indistinguishable shift from nihilism to whatever its opposite might appropriately be called, Arthur summons to him a young page, a boy who reveals that he hopes to *kill* as many of the enemy as possible in the next day's climactic encounter. Instead of letting the boy kill, Arthur knights him and tells him to go forth as a vessel for the mighty idea which in Arthur's generation had so miserably failed. He will not let the boy taste the battle nor remember the past, for the England he sends him back to is kingless and idealless. Mordred and the knights of the Round Table will be dead, Arthur will be dead, and Lancelot and Guenever will be eternal recluses. Arthur needs the boy to take the dream back in its purest form, untainted by any notion of Might or "Right," no matter whether "is" or "for" occurs between those questionably capitalized words. Arthur himself had tried to instill purity and virtue in men who were, himself included, corrupted by the inscrutable past, by self-love, and by war as the logical means to obliterate the first and gratify the second. This page will speak to a new breed of people, unschooled in any of these; for all three characteristics are to annihilate themselves on the following day. As Arthur realizes this fact, he seems to feel the spirit of Merlyn pass near him—and, of course, it has.

On the final page of the novel, Arthur, now the once and future king, changes from a character with an ideal into the very symbol of the ideal: "There would be a day—there must be a day—when he would come back to Gramarye with a new Round Table which had no corners, just as the world had none—a table without boundaries between the nations who would sit to feast there. The hope of making it would lie in culture. If people could be persuaded to read and write, not just to eat and make love, there was still a chance that they might come to reason" (676). And the novel itself concludes with the following words:

EXPLICIT LIBER REGIS QUONDAM REGISQUE FUTURI

(The book of the once king and the king of the future unfolds)

THE BEGINNING

CHAPTER 5

The Neoclassicist

I Mistress Masham's Repose

MISTRESS *Masham's Repose* (1946), a novel not without its flaws but one of White's finest, marks his transition during the early 1940's from medievalist to neoclassicist, from Arthurian to Swiftian, and from philosopher and theologian to Juvenalian satirist and scandalmonger. White's later affection for this novel was limited, for it was the one he was working on when Brownie died on November 25, 1944. He considered the initial version of the book "sound," but Garnett's reaction (very favorable to the initial idea) was full of dissonance: "You have stumbled upon a most beautiful subject and you have the opportunity of writing a masterpiece. But you have not stopped to think, and instead of writing a masterpiece you have filled it up with a lot of twaddle about Miss Pribble and the Vicar, those stock clowns."[1]

White humbly submitted to this adverse criticism, for he knew himself to have been concerned with other, less important things while writing the novel, such as pursuing in Inniskea the object recounted in *The Godstone and the Blackymor*, translating the ever-present bestiary, and, of course, grieving over Brownie's death. Also he devoted too much space in the novel to the architecture (copied from Stowe) of Malplaquet, Maria's home in the book. Despite Garnett's somewhat justified reaction, the novel, first published in America and in England a year later, enjoyed a good measure of success in both countries. In 1947, White refused to sell the film rights, despite a good price offered. He did, in fact, make enough money from this book to force him to move to the Channel island of Alderney to avoid paying any more taxes on the proceeds from the book upon which the United States had also collected a good deal.

The book was dedicated to Garnett's baby daughter, Amaryllis

Virginia; and at one point or another the novel was almost released under any one of several more descriptive titles: *Lilliput in Exile*, *Lie Low*, *Lilliput*, and even *As Yahoos Like It*. In White's several novels built around already established literary constructs, he tends either to reinterpret (as in the Arthurian books) or to expand the subject matter of its original creator as in *Mistress Masham's Repose*. This novel is an extension upon Swift's "A Voyage to Lilliput," the first book of *Gulliver's Travels*. When, according to Swift, Gulliver set sail from Blefuscu, he was picked up by an English vessel commanded by a Captain John Biddel. Initiating one of the central themes of the novel even before the temporal span of the book itself begins, White decided that Biddel, after hearing Gulliver rave about the little people and such, could not resist finding Lilliput for himself. Thus, White's extension of the Gulliver story is based upon this portion of a Swift paragraph:

> This gentleman [Biddel] treated me with kindness and desired I would let him know what place I came from last, and whither I was bound; which I did in a few words, but he thought I was raving, and that the dangers I underwent had disturbed my head; whereupon I took my black cattle and sheep out of my pocket, which, after great astonishment, clearly convinced him of my veracity. I then showed him the gold given me by the Emperor of Blefuscu, together with his Majesty's picture at full length, and some other rarities of that country. I gave him two purses of two hundred *sprugs* each, and promised, when we arrived in England, to make him a present of a cow and a sheep big with young.[2]

In the next paragraph we find Gulliver remarking without concern about Biddel's kindness in keeping the tiny animals alive. It seems on the surface that, for Swift, Biddel is one of the few kind men the human race supplies. White suggests, in *Mistress Masham's Repose*, that Swift knew better; Biddel, having unloaded the naive Gulliver in England, sailed back to the proper latitude as quickly as possible because of the desire for the money which such miniatures would bring being too much for him or any man to cope with. (Even Gulliver charged admission to see his animals and then sold them for six hundred pounds.)

And so, in the seventh chapter, White presents the story of

Biddel's return through his spokesman the Lilliputian Schoolmaster whom Maria discovers (along with the rest of his colony) on an island on the Malplaquet estate. Hoping to inspire caution in the young girl, the Schoolmaster relates that Gulliver's inability to keep quiet had allowed Biddel to find them so easily. Both Lilliput and Blefuscu (people of both reside on Mistress Masham's Repose) had been particularly vulnerable at the time of Biddel's arrival; for, antagonized by such points of difference as the Big Endian controversy and the fact that the Blefuscans had allowed the Man Mountain to escape, the two tiny nations had been at war. Biddel had had little trouble selecting as many humans and animals as he liked and taking them to England for profit. The Schoolmaster's estimate of Biddel's character states clearly the over-riding theme of White's novel:

> "Captain Biddel, Ma'am, according to our Annals, was a Seaman of his Era and Country, neither better nor worse than others of his Rank. To him, Ma'am, and, I must beg Leave to add with honest Gratitude that we have found no Occasion as yet to notice such a Disposition in Yourself, to him our broken and distrackted people were Creatures not possessed of human Rights, nor shelter'd by the Laws of Nations. Our Cattle were for his Profit, because we could not defend them; our very Persons were an Object of Cupidity, for he had determined to show us in his native Land, as Puppet Shews and Mimes." (52)[3]

Biddel, it is crucial for us to note, was "neither better nor worse" than any other man—but greed and lust had taken command of him. He had packed human and beast alike in a box and had hauled them thousands of miles across the sea and then from town to town to display them at gin shops and at country fairs. One night, however, the corpulent Biddel, who had taken heavily to drink, fell from his horse on the road near Malplaquet. Having forgotten to lock the box in which the Lilliputians were carried and being too drunk to realize what was happening, Biddel lost his Lilliputians when they escaped and assumed residence on the unkept, thicketed little island in the middle of the Quincunx on the grounds of Malplaquet. Here they had lived for nearly two hundred and fifty years before Maria accidentally discovered their civilization, known to them as Lilliput in Exile.

The story of *Mistress Masham's Repose*, then, is about one of the Lilliputians who is trying to escape a similar fate not only from Maria but more terrifyingly from the designs of the novel's stock villains, Miss Brown, Maria's guardian, and the local parson, Vicar Hater. Throughout, White maintains a level of discourse amazingly close to Swift's: the overlying tone of innocence and the underlying permeation of evil are welded satirically together in such a way that *Mistress Masham's Repose* could be, as *Gulliver's Travels* often has been called, a story for children. Like Swift's classic, however, it is not.

Like Swift's work as well, much of the stock nonsense which often overclutters the surface must be penetrated to the not-so-stock, not-so-nonsensical content which is concealed beneath it. Garnett called Miss Brown and the Vicar "twaddle," and it is hard to defend White since these characters develop almost too obviously from kind of bad people into very bad people—from thieves of money and property (Maria's inheritance) to thieves of human rights and dignity (the Lilliputians'). At the end of the novel, they are even overdeveloped when they consider, first, starving Maria and the Professor to death in a dungeon, and second, murdering them immediately (something of which even they did not seem capable throughout the story). Moreover, they even *look* like villains: the vicar is short, has a red face rifled with hundreds of tiny blue veins, eyes which lurk behind thick spectacles, greasy hair which is combed flat and parted in the middle. Miss Brown has a hawk-face on a pudgy body, her hair is yellow and drawn in a bun, and she wears a pince-nez. Not only does she plot to relieve Maria of her estate, but she also melts the heroine's chocolates in an oven "to purify them." She is not a nice lady, and Vicar Hater is not a nice man. Both, as Garnett said so well, are "twaddle."

Not only do they look like stock villains, desire like stock villains, but they also perform like stock villains. Having discovered the gifts that the People give Maria and thinking that they were found in an undiscovered room in the house, Miss Brown (the originator of the evil schemes who once again resembles White's mother) and the parasitical Hater in progressive order send Maria to bed supperless for not revealing where she obtained the loot, stop the sympathetic Cook from bringing her food, spring in upon Maria when the Lilliputians arrive with victuals, capture (and shortly lose) the Schoolmaster, set Maria free in order to follow her to the People's home, are led into innumerable dead ends and resultant arguments by the crafty young girl (very funny, if slapsticklike, scenes), lock Maria up in a medieval dungeon until she tattles on her friends, capture the friends when they arrive on rafts to free their protectress, are outsmarted by the purer minds of the less corruptible, and eventually are put in jail to torture each other with "if only's" for the rest of their lives. Such are the vehicles that convey the more important considerations of the book.

The overdrawn evil of Brown and Hater tends to overshadow the possibility for evil, particularly greed and the desire for some measure of power over other human beings, which both Swift and White discover with dismay to exist even in the very normal person. Maria, for example, though only ten years old, hardly knows the Lilliputians at all before (realizing that they seem to trust her and, especially, that she is bigger than they) she becomes a tyrant and uses the poor things as toy soldiers and as guinea pigs in various experiments. She takes favorites, attempts to make others jealous, and tries in every way to dominate. To young to be corrupted by money, she is old enough to inate. Too young to be corrupted by money, she is old enough to take them. She comes to assume that the People cannot live without her—one night, while they are whale (pike) hunting, she, in an effort to help them, sinks the fish they have laboriously brought in tow. When, on another occasion, she almost kills a man by making him pilot a rubber-band-powered model airplane, she is ordered to leave the island. Even earlier, however, she was somewhat guilty of the same thing Brown and Hater are. Upon her first arrival on the island, seeing the baby in the walnut shell and resenting its mother's attempt to protect it, she kidnaps the two of them because of her curiosity and because of her size since she demonstrates that she is bigger and need not endure the prick of Lilliputian harpoons.

The turning point in the book comes, therefore, when Maria is sufficiently educated in ethics to realize that the duty of the bigger person is to be protective rather than opportunistic. Ninety percent of this education is accomplished during two sessions with her friend the Professor who seems to be a critical portrait of White himself. Written during the years when White was laboring over *The Bestiary,* this novel portrays a scholar more interested in the exact translation of one obscure medieval Latin word than in the entire fantastic series of events that continually threatens to overwhelm him. To become interested in a person's problems, he must literally be jolted to awareness of mundane concerns. Maria finally manages to make clear to him her problem concerning friendship with the People, and the Professor *is* able to make one thing clear about the old theme of might and right. When Maria complains that the captured lady provides no "fun," he observes that people who are captured and contained by bigger people usually do not: "'. . . Well, then, Maria, although this is not a fashionable way of going on, nor even a successful one, it is a thing which I believe in—that people must not tyrannize, nor try to be great because they are little. My dear, you are a great person yourself, in any case, and you do not need to lord it over others, in order to prove your greatness'" (29).

Maria's tendency to bully is cured, but possessiveness (already alluded to) is dealt with by the Professor several chapters later. Using Gulliver's relationship with the Brobdingnagian girl Glumdalclitch as an archetype, he instructs the vain little child:

> ". . . It was because she did not paw him about [that they got on well]. Don't you remember how disgusted he was by the other young ladies who tried to make him a play thing? He hated being mauled and messed, and he was grateful to Glumdalclitch because she only behaved as a loving attendant and helper. This is what you will have to do, if you want to make it up with Lilliput. You must never, never force them to do anything. . . . When they see your magnanimity in not exerting brute force, they will admire you and give you love." (83)

Maria subdues her pride and returns to the loving embrace of the Schoolmaster; despite a bit of backsliding here and there in theory more than in action, Maria is as reformed as it is possible for human beings, who innately possess the vices of which White and Swift write, to be.

The Professor, despite his sage advice to Maria, is never totally above such behavior himself; but his attempts at possession are obliquely tempered by what he preaches. Rather than capture, use, and possess tiny, defenseless Lilliputians, the Professor has illusions of conquering a big, more-powerful-than-he Brobdingnagian. The fact that the little man could win seems to relieve some immorality and that he would treat him kindly mitigates, for the Professor at least, his intent. He forgets and never realizes that Maria also thought she was being nice and that the only benefit from such a plan would be his. The Professor, despite his foibles, is one of the soundest human beings that White has portrayed; but he is also as human, in the deprecatory sense of the word, as anyone else. The seemingly clear lines drawn between the horrid villains and the victorious heroes thus become, as they do in so many White books, grayer.

If White is examining flaws in these particular human beings as well as in human nature in general, he also relates what he has to say, from the novel's opening page, to England. Long critical of countries that try to dominate other countries,[4] White seems to be fashioning Malplaquet into a microcosmic England in order to demonstrate how the vices that all men possess and those that are cultivated by Brown and Hater have infested an entire nation. He compares Maria's estate to Buckingham Palace in the book's second paragraph, and he then mentions that it and its tradition are crumbling. The girl who is to inherit it will have little of which to be proud, since not only is her inheritance full of physical decay but also its moral reputation has been ruined by previous owners who have squandered the family wealth through overextension and pretentiousness.

The wreck is ruled by the Vicar—the Church and false morality—and by Miss Brown, the symbol of staid, inhuman traditionalism, who, in her effort to keep the land "pure" and conservatively productive, stifles the rights and the very growth of those who are to follow her. Practical goodness and sound principles (the Cook and the Professor) are consigned to near poverty and to ineffectual positions. Through the presence of the Lilliputians, White appears to be criticizing the manner in which England colonizes for its own good and leaves the people whose condition it intended, theoretically at least, to improve living in the equivalent of slums and primitivism. The falsity and insecurity of this situation White symbolizes excellently in the dungeon sequence in which the Professor and the People, discovering Maria to be imprisoned, look with historical reflection upon the great door and lock. Every great monarch's reign produced some elaboration upon this instrument of human torture; yet, when the Professor decides that the dungeon must be entered, he merely removes the hinges of the door, and the great tradition is shattered. More than writing a limited satire on the lust and greed of mankind, White is voicing a wish that England as a country might realize how insecure are the entities it has valued in the past and emerge with new, more moral, more humanistic values.

This criticism, through satire, frequently becomes more specific. Concerning religion, he shows Mr. Hater's retaining the captured Schoolmaster in the box which holds offerings for the Society for the Propagation of Christian Knowledge. About parliamentary government, the Professor wonders at one point why one does not have to pass an examination to become a lawmaker. The police and legalism are hit rather hard when the Professor, who attempts to save Maria from murder, is frustrated by a disinterested policeman and by the mountain of paperwork which would have to be completed before one life could be saved. On taxes, White is equally blunt; for his own living conditions were shortly to be changed in order to save himself from the taxes of two countries: one of the reasons the Professor feels the Lilliputians should not be listed as citizens of England, deserving of its benevolence and protection, is that they would be taxed far in excess of the four hundred sprugs they possess. Also, once having revealed themselves, they would have to go to the courts to protect themselves against kidnappers, and this procedure would cost even more money. In other words, from White's viewpoint, no relationship exists between taxes and government benefits,

However, a similarity of view does not always exist between White and Swift. For one thing, White is far more tolerant of the Lilliputians than Swift is; but White may be so because the Lilliputians, having now endured two-and-one-half centuries of adversity, are a more stable and less petty race. The English, having had good fortune, are still what Swift thought them to be in his own day. Lilliput in Exile is an industrious society and an extremely happy one because everyone is what he wants to be—there are no conventions to constrain him. The Lilliputians establish their culture and maintain it at a practical level (even reducing the number of syllables in a heroic couplet so they may better write one) rather than trying to seem greater than they are. They are poor and suspicious, but these characteristics are not their fault.

One excellent contrast between the good Lilliputian and the good Englishman occurs during the scene in which all are trying to escape the grip of Miss Brown. The little people are trying to unbolt the huge dungeon door, while the Professor is searching through some Latin inscriptions, looking, as he has been during most of the book's critical events, for the meaning of one Latin word—*"tripharium."* In Swiftian terms, the Professor is a Laputan—one so engaged in theoretical pursuits that he is helpless in practical ones; but we should also remember that the Professor was the one who *thought* to remove the hinges! White raises an interesting question which again prevents a static appraisal of either side when, in a convincing remonstrance to Maria, the Professor defends Laputa by saying that Swift was wrong to mock people who think:

> "You see, Maria, this world is run by 'practical' people; that is to say by people who do not know how to think, have never had any education in thinking, and who do not wish to have it. They get on far better with lies, tub thumping, swindling, vote-catching, murdering and the rest of practical politics. So, when a person who can think does come along, to tell them what they are doing wrong or how to put it right, they have to invent some way of slinging mud at him, for fear of losing their power and being forced to do the right thing. . . . I don't believe that a thinking man like Dr. Swift ought to have helped the practical politicians, by poking fun at the thinkers, even if he only meant to poke fun at the silly ones. Time is revenging itself upon the Dean. It is bringing in, as real inventions, the very ones which he made up for ridicule." (180–81)

White is trying for more than a cut-and-dried dichotomy in this novel; he is implying, I think, that neither the practical nor the theoretical can profitably exist by itself. Generally, people are practical; and practicality eventually, if left untempered, produces selfishness which yields to greed. The Lilliputians represent pure, tempered practicality which the unreality of their situation prevents from walking the other two steps downward. Their practicality is expressly designed to offset the selfishness and greed that the practicality of others has produced. The Professor, on the other hand, is purely theoretical; but he can hardly keep alive for want of practicality—and White regards himself as such a person. What is needed is the impossible blend, and this combination is what draws both the People and the Professor to Maria. She is not yet in perfect blend, but she is the only character in the novel who is headed in the right direction. The concluding chapter, though overly sentimental, emphasizes this fact. The microcosm of Malplaquet, so torn with greed and fear at the outset, now gravitates blissfully around the new Maria, and both the Professor and the Lilliputians derive from her an eighteenth-century sense of balance and order.

If this analysis has made *Mistress Masham's Repose* seem a very philosophical work, it has done so because of the novel's deceiving simplicity—much in the way that other critical discussions affect a concept of *Gulliver's Travels*. The surface of White's work, though, is not to be taken lightly, for it contains many good things. Indicating how White approaches a subject, he spends several chapters discussing and estimating the difficulties that six-inch people would have in everyday living in a six-foot society. This discernment is reminiscent of his tremendous insights into medieval knight-errantry in *The Sword in the Stone* and his forthcoming feeling for a goshawk wrapped in a bag. White's imagination functions at its best as he portrays Lilliputians riding rats as horses, trying to train birds to be airplanes, and being attacked by foxes and grass snakes. White has a supreme talent for recognizing the humorous even in the most precarious situations.

Some of the book's humor and satire are even more surreptitiously included, however. Various eighteenth-century allusions are strewn throughout the novel, and he later repeats many of them in his twin books about this century which so fascinated him in the late 1940's. For example, White satirizes the printing techniques of the eighteenth century every time a Lilliputian speaks—he speaks in capitals. Once White remarks that Maria must have been glad to have a long tale by the Schoolmaster reach its climax, for her head was buzzing with capital letters. Another stab at printing is contained in his version of the title page from Gulliver's Lilliputian dictionary, for the sheet abounds with subordinate clauses in a hundred-word title. Here and there, again as was the practice two centuries ago, White the narrator speaks directly to "Amaryllis," the child to whom the book is dedicated. He even resembles Laurence Sterne in *Tristam Shandy* in his use of stranded punctuation marks, such as the paragraph composed only of a question mark (33). In the "Scandal" books, White uses archaic spelling throughout the works to lend a bit of extra flavor to his study, but its limited use in the novel remains humorous and never assumes the tediousness that his later attempt eventually does.

The novel is also full of riotous comedy. The Vicar and Miss Brown chase Maria through thickets and bogs in quest of the home of the little people. When they climb 365 steps into a tower, thinking Maria has gone to the top, they seem more like fools than the potentially dangerous people they are. White caps the scene by having Maria lock them in for the night and then quietly unlock the door in the morning, causing both to think that it had been open all the while. This prank precipitates, of course, one of the continual sessions of bickering that the Vicar and his beloved endure.

Mistress Masham's Repose is a success, despite some rather important flaws. The villains are types. The Lilliputians have little substance to them—the Schoolmaster, for example, is a good man, but it is hard to determine just why he is so. Throughout the book, the presence of six-inch men and women is a little too taken for granted by most characters; and such acceptance diminishes some of the realism that the novel needs to emphasize the stature of its considerations—in short, the substance of what is being said is often shielded too much by the ingenuity of White's inventions. In the last chapter, a Christmas party—after all bad people are jailed and all good people are joined together—is almost totally pointless; and it emphasizes once again the trouble White has in constructing firm and meaningful conclusions for novels which have led his imagination hither and yon (his next book, *The Elephant and the Kangaroo*, makes this weakness even more apparent). On the whole, however, next to the Arthurian tetralogy, *Mistress Masham's Repose* is likely to remain White's most popular work of fiction.

II The Elephant and the Kangaroo

The Elephant and the Kangaroo, published in America in 1947 and in England a year later, is White's funniest novel and, at the same time, one of his most intolerant. The book is about an English atheist, *a* Mr. White, who lives in Ireland during World War II. White is obviously T. H. White, for the hero has done all the things the author did in his life, and both the hero and the author have dogs named Brownie. The hero is always spoken about in the third person, however, mainly because this narrative method gives White the opportunity to satirize himself (which he does continually) rather than just Ireland alone. Mr. White's landlords, an elderly couple called the O'Callaghans (obviously the McDonaghs) are, to quote Sylvia Warner, ragbags "of the Christian virtues and a Noble Savage."[6]

One day the Archangel Michael comes down the O'Callaghans' chimney[6] to tell them about the advent of the Second Flood, which is shortly to inundate the world. Mr. White and the O'Callaghans are told to build an ark, collect animals, and in other ways prepare for the catastrophe. The O'Callaghans, "devout" Christians though they are, are immediately skeptical, not because they doubt the veracity of what the angel has told them, but because the whole project would demand more work and discipline than had ever been demanded of them before. Nonbeliever White, however, is stunned by the revelation; and he immediately begins the project but has little or no help from his holier landlords. With the aid of a suspicious townsman (who is never told what is happening), Mr. White overturns the O'Callaghans' barn to serve as the shell of his ark. He builds compartments for animals, food, and essential items for starting a new world—books and hundreds of other items which are suggested during nightly list-making sessions.

Throughout, Mr. White, who is conscious of his enormous responsibility in determining the course of history in the new world, often feels impelled to make moral decisions about such otherwise unimportant matters as whether a still should be included on the ark. Even more important is the fact that he is unable to obtain elephants, tigers, lions, and every animal not immediately available in Ireland; in order that those of the new civilization might know what they are, he packs an encyclopedia which even he feels is a poor substitute. White, faithful to what the angel has told him to do, is constantly at odds with his elderly landlords, simply because they have no conception about what a Flood, with a capital 'F," entails. Their faith in God's goodness usually allows them to look beyond the very messenger of Doom that God has sent them.

Finally, while the project is still uncompleted, the rain begins. Mr. White collects all on the ark just in time, for the boat is quick to set sail with the swift current. Nothing is in order, and the ark has its top shaved off by the first low bridge. Five miles later it is impaled on another and begins to sink. Realizing that all is lost, the ark-builder ties three barrels together in the shape of the ace of clubs; puts himself, the O'Callaghans, and Brownie into them; and uses his raft as a lifeboat to abandon ship. Once in the barrels, however, they find themselves unable to steer and consequently unable to get to the shore of the river into which the Flood has taken them. On top of this problem, the barrels are constantly spinning around; moreover, they are being followed by hundreds of townspeople who, hitherto untrusting, feel now that the best way to salvation is to sail, in anything that is available, after Mr. White and his ragged crew. Rumors begin to fly across the countryside (which seemingly is not about to be so inundated as the archangel had predicted); and, by the time the entourage passes through Dublin, the Irish military has braced itself for a reported invasion. Because of the ineptitude of the army and navy, Mr. White and his followers survive the resistance, float out to sea, and are picked up by a mailboat. There was one more chapter intended, presumably to include Mr. White's attempt at self-justification, but at Garnett's recommendation this section was excluded from the published novel.

The Irish were infuriated by this book, but they seem to have overlooked the fact that Mr. White, the author himself, is the first and foremost object of satire. After all, it is entirely his doing that toward the end of the book, half the Irish countryside is following him in barrels along an overflowing river. Throughout, the hero is pictured as a man who, although considerate and ingenious, is overly philosophic and slightly addlepated. Despite the superstitious devotion of the Irish to every piece of legend they know, the O'Callaghans suspect the angel's message from the very first; but Mr. White, on the other hand, changes his religious position. Although the story leads the reader to believe that his transmutation took place on account of his constant existence in the Irish stratosphere, his duping is still complete. In the course of several minutes he switches from one who believes that creation was a process of spontaneous combustion to one who trusts God to alleviate every insoluble problem, if not now, at least when the Flood comes. Mr. White's flaw seems to be that he has entertained himself too often with purely theoretical reasonings, almost theory for the sake of theory; and, when his spontaneous combustion idea disintegrates with the appearance of the angel, he is too quick to latch on to a new, now more promising idea—"he was able to adjust his ideas to the new basis with scarcely any alteration" (34).[7]

Mr. White is satirized even more severely every time he criticizes the Irish during the narrative. What the offended readers failed to realize was that the hero was actually more involved in superstition than the very people he continually accused of it. And, at the very moment Mr. White is most scornful about the inability of the Irish to do anything correctly, he discovers that he has forgotten to include a woman capable of bearing children —thus, though various worms and amoebae will survive in his new world, the human race cannot.

In the long run, however, the satire of the Irish is the funniest and the most interesting part of the book; but the Irish themselves are really only microcosmic. White does not attempt to disguise this fact since he makes this statement early in the novel:

> For that matter, what is the good of doing anything with the Irish, who won't even try water divining? What are they? Just a rag bag of every defeated nation since the dawn of prehistory, driven into this accursed rain-cloud of an island as the last refuge for incapacity. They think that the sunlight puts fires out and the moon changes the weather and God knows what else. I suppose they think that the moon

is a kind of phosphorescent balloon which gets gradually blown up and deflated. They have no idea of the earth's shadow or of geography or of anything else. The only good thing is that they murder one another at a great rate. (78)

But late in the novel commentary about the Irish has changed to a general statement about man's lot:

How desperately cruel life is, thought Mr. White: Life and Time. They take everything, take the soft-petaled maiden and the fashions she pondered. Fashion and slang are awful in their pathos. There are spinsters knocking about nowadays, I suppose, who cry girlishly that such and such a thing is 'some stunt' and who would like to describe themselves as 'flappers'. In twenty years the Wrens of to-day will be saying 'browned off' with the same cracked ring. Human beings run about like sheep, copying one another, talking the latest idiom, wearing the latest hat. And Time comes stealthily to rob them, till idiom and hat are both ridiculous, leaving nothing in the little squirrel hoard of graces. (157)

Once again, that inscrutable, hazy Power which ultimately arrives to accept the blame in many of White's novels has appeared in this one as well. The Irish escape blame much as Lancelot and even Mordred do in the tetralogy.

The excellence of *The Elephant and the Kangaroo* lies mainly in the fact that even the Irishmen that White creates are never stereotypes. Even the term "Irish" does not have attached to it its usual connotations. Mrs. O'Callaghan is probably the best example of the Irish psyche—in any event, she is the symbol of everything Irish for the raging Mr. White. Although a woman who attributes every moment to the Love and Providence of God, her first (and last) reaction to the archangel, whom she continually refers to as "she," is that it will hurt them. Her entire religion, in fact, is nothing but picture-book superstitions which never fail to frustrate Mr. White. Mr. White summarizes their very "metaphysical" discussion of the Holy Ghost in this way:

"Good. Now we are getting along. Now we are beginning to know where we stand. There is a certain pigeon, *Columba oenas*, which flies in the stratosphere head downwards, with its wings at an angle of incidence of ninety degrees, with a piece of paper in its beak and some rays proceeding from its body in all directions, and this pigeon is known as the Holy Ghost, and anybody who refuses to believe such stuff and nonsense will forthwith be consigned to the depths of Hell, which is a place of real fire, and there he will be tortured by a benevolent deity, for ever and ever and ever?" (203)

To this statement, Mrs. O'Callaghan agrees. At another point Mr. White spends pages trying to convince her of the extent of a "Flood," something she never comprehends. Moreover, her views are a bundle of contradictions. Though insistence upon God's infallibility is a tenet of her life and religion, she is nonetheless able, when confronted with the distasteful reality of a Flood, to state that "'*everybody* makes mistakes sometimes'" (111). Her greatest proof of the existence of God is His omnipotence; yet, when Mr. White tells her that they will have to depend on the will of God to populate the new world (since he has forgotten to bring a wife), she anxiously remarks: "'But God... doesn't be able to do anything which is not *possible*, Mr. White.'" To which White, demonstrating long residence in Ireland, replies: "'Everything is possible to God'" (129).

Author White, who once almost became a Catholic himself, is even more pointedly satiric about Irish Catholicism.[8] To the individuals in this novel, their religion seems to be more a voodoo curse than a doctrine of love. Wicked things might happen to a Catholic who failed to say his prayers, or more explicitly, favors just might not be granted. Thus, no matter what an Irish Catholic was doing, his act was always permeated by a pragmatic "love" of God. When the ark sets sail, the residents of Burkestown "howled out the rosary, and shook their fists" (151). Even Father Byrne, the local priest who seems to generate new superstitions and to stabilize old ones whenever they suit his purpose, shakes his fist at Mr. White during the recitation of the Litany of the Virgin when he sees the Englishman assuming the role of Savior for the desperate town. If prayer, in these cases, is a time to invoke the wrath of God upon an enemy, for the gentler Mrs. O'Callaghan it is a time to think about other worldly problems. Catholicism *qua* Catholicism, then, is a license to live rather than a doctrine to which the Irish Catholic should physically and spiritually commit himself. When Catholicism seems no longer likely to allow survival, the entire Irish countryside jumps into anything that floats and follows the spinning Mr. White downstream toward the new world. He, rather than Christ, is now the Savior.

Religion is just one of many things at which the Irish are totally inept—according to the exasperated Mr. White. Mikey O'Callaghan lets entire flocks and herds die by leaving them unfed in the winter, and he loses entire harvests by failing to reap them in time. Mrs. O'Callaghan is entirely incompetent as a homemaker, and White feels that only the grace of God permits the family to exist at all. When a farm laborer attempts to murder Mr. White (the man feels that White is building an ark just to make fools of the town), he fires a pistol at the back of the ark-builder's neck, and "It was lucky for the ark that they were Irish cartridges" (126).

During the hilarious regatta of barrels and bathtubs at the end of the novel, the author catalogues ineptitude upon Irish ineptitude. A local constable wires to Dublin that the country has been invaded by river by Abyssinians. Despite the fact that Irish communications consists of only four telephones and three wireless sets, the Irish navy and air force are readied for the "invaders'" passage through Dublin. But, alas, there are only two planes in the air force; one cannot get off the ground, and the other is forced to fly at fifteen thousand feet to avoid all sorts of rumored disasters:

Submarines, parachutists, blackamoors, Freemasons, spies, the I.R.A., the Ku Klux Klan, Mr. Black and Tans, Orangemen, and a landing of the Eskimos, had been freely reported. From coast to coast of Eriu, lighthouse-keepers were peering out to sea, stationmasters were puzzling over telegraph forms, Guarda sergeants were issuing three rounds of ball, inspectors of this and that were gazing at the sky, museum officials were hiding the Cross of Cong, Catholic boy scouts were hitching up their little belts, typists were pattering directives, old-age pensioners were concealing their bankbooks, members of the stock exchange were fingering grubby scapulars, and at least ten thousand of the faithful were making mental vows to advertise their thanks to the newspapers, if spared, to Blessed Oliver Plunkett, Matt Talbot, The Little Flower, St. Philomena, St. Anthony of Padua, the Infant of Prague, Our Lady of Lourdes, and to other worthies too numerous to be mentioned. (209)

When the fleet passes through Dublin, the Irish Army fires upon it. When the soldiers fire high, they smash the newly washed portholes in the ships of the Irish Navy: "The personnel of the Irish Navy, incensed by having had to clean the portholes for nothing, suspicious of treachery, and infuriated by the fright they had received, drew their boy-scout pocket knives and plunged into the Liffey. They were going to swim across and cut the guts out of the Army, or perish in the attempt" (217). In short, according to Mr. White, the Irish can do nothing, absolutely nothing, right.

The book's funniest moment comes when New Savior White, ashamed of himself and of the country for following him, actually assumes the Savior role in an attempt to disperse the armada of fear- and faith-driven apostles:

> He instantly leaped up again, and began shaking his fist at the congregation.
>
> "Go away!" he screamed. "Get out of the river! Clear out! The Flood's off. Damn you, the Flood's off!" (195–96)

Indeed, the book is good fun if one is not an Irishman without a sense of humor; but morals are to be derived, and no characters exist with whom we can (or dare to) identify. The workman who dubiously helps Mr. White build the Ark, Pat Geraghty, is a somewhat antithetical Irishman who refuses to let anyone else work on a project because he fears that he will do it incorrectly. All the work Mr. White does in the construction is ripped up by the perfunctory Geraghty to do it over again. Geraghty is one of the neighborhood *maniacs* (lots of these in Ireland); but, as one of the safer ones, he suffers only from delusions of grandeur rather than from sexual perversion or from other more intolerable vices. Another man, Tommy Plunkett, who has been mildly reprimanded by the district judge for infanticide, does all field work on the O'Callaghan farm. A young girl servant, Philomena, steals from Mr. White and takes the stolen items home to her twenty-three brothers and sisters. She is suspected of having strangled her first-born child (illegitimate) and of burying him in a box beneath an inch of top soil. This event caused horror in the neighborhood around Burkestown, for the makeshift coffin was quickly dug up by a local dog. The headlines in the newspaper told the story: "DISGRACEFUL BEHAVIOR OF DOG" (30).

There is, as we mentioned earlier, very little thematic core to the novel. Even the building of the Ark recedes at times far into the background when something occurs which allows the nervous Mr. White a chance to vent his spleen upon some Irishman or Irish custom. At odds with the wildness of the Irish civilization is the calm reserve with which Mr. White approaches crucial situations. Both his confrontation with Archangel Michael and his reception of the information that the world is to be destroyed are reserved and apparently rational, almost resigned. When the rain comes, his embarkation is unceremonious—he just gathers his flock and boards. Only when the Ark is wrecked five miles from Burkestown does he begin to suspect that he has somehow been taken—God protected Noah from shipwreck, didn't He? His ride in the barrels shows his change from a submissive believer to an embarrassed atheist once again. Of course, a fabulistic story such as this one does not deal with the reasons that caused a mistake to be made, if indeed it *was* a mistake. Possibly the atmosphere that produces Irish superstition finally overtook Mr. White's senses or possibly there really was an archangel in the chimney; but the question should probably be left unanswered since the novel itself makes no attempt to drop hints.

What *The Elephant and the Kangaroo definitely* is, however, is an artist's reaction to years of supersition and seemingly irrational custom. The whole wild melee is set forth in this very light and comical book, and no morals or solutions are offered or recommended. White again investigates these same years in Ireland in the series of analytic vignettes published twelve years later, *The Godstone and the Blackymor*. In this work he attempts in a serious way to penetrate to the core of these people who so amused and so exasperated him.

III The Age of Scandal

The Age of Scandal, which White often called his "Horry Walpole book," was published in June, 1950, though it was another of his long-term efforts, its conception dating from the weeks before Brownie's death in late 1944. The majority of White's scholarly research and the composition seems to have taken place at Doolistown in 1945, but the book was not completed until mid-1948. This year, however, witnessed one of White's worst drinking spells; and the book had to be shaken loose by Garnett. Upon publication, White was somewhat concerned about it; for, as he told Garnett, the first book was too cruel—cruel enough to prevent readers from proceeding to its more sedate sequel, *The Scandalmonger* (1952).

The Age of Scandal dates from the period in White's life when research and scholarship seemed suddenly to intrigue him, for its composition was contemporaneous with that of *The Bestiary*, another such work. The book's very general topic seems to be the climate of the second half of the eighteenth century, and the volume itself is composed of sixteen sketches of the people and the fads which composed it. Unlike most books about eighteenth-century England, its heroes are Horace Walpole and Lord Sporus Hervey; and its villain is Alexander Pope. White states his somewhat purposefully eccentric thesis in this fashion:

> I believe that the peak of British culture was reached in the latter years of George II: that the rot began to set in with the "Romantics": that the apparent prosperity of Victoria's reign was autumnal, not vernal: and that now we are done for.
>
> I have been consoling my old age by running away from the Bondfields and the Shinwells and the Bevans, by going back to the grand old days of Horace Walpole, and I have written this book in the effort to give one last, loving and living picture of an aristocratic civilization which we shall never see again. (17)[9]

And the "Age of Scandal" itself, an era whose boundaries have been established by White's fanciful interests, is defined as follows:

> Between the Classical and the Romantic movements, as they are recognized at present, there existed this other age, which was one of peculiar flavour. It filled the hiatus between Pope and Wordsworth with a distinct and unique culture, nonetheless real because it is seldom recognized now. It could be roughly dated between the death of Pope and the publication of the Lyrical Ballads, except that such

> dates are confusing. Periods do not exist between fixed years. They have forerunners in the previous age and laggards in the subsequent one. Although the Age of Scandal was at its height in the seventeen-eighties, under its greatest product, Horace Walpole, yet, between forerunner and laggard, it may be said to have stretched from Lady Mary Wortley Montagu to Croker or to Creevey. (23)

White spends pages enumerating the qualities necessary to be a bona fide member of the age, but the lowest common denominator seems to be a sort of mischievousness that the Age of Reason was too reasonable and that the Age of Romanticism was too transcendental to permit. The era's zest for gossip and for all things below board makes it for White—as he proceeds in two volumes to make it for his reader—the most colorful, the most humorous, and, at the same time, the most potentially frightening epoch in history.

The brevity of White's introduction to the "Age of Scandal" is justified by its ability to speak for itself. The first sketch, entitled *"Agremens"*—the measure of the English interests in the 1780's—attempts in a somewhat disorganized manner to display the comfortable pleasures to which this seemingly all-leisure-class age was addicted. The picture presented is too incoherently drawn to be as vivid as subsequent ones, but White has made it clear that the age had certain customs which were "in" for any man (or woman) of parts. Such a personage had to speak slowly and move gracefully, almost as if performing in a ballet. He had to eat his dinner slowly, converse at the table for long hours afterward (some of which time was to be spent discussing indecent subjects), drink heavily, and climax it all with a delicate and dignified drink of "tay." He was, if the opportunity arose, to experiment in fanciful medicines to prevent those discomforts which comfortable society found uncomfortable. He was, at all times, to separate himself, by appearance and carriage, from the grosser Frenchman, among whom, according to Dr. Johnson, "a lady . . . will spit on the floor, and rub it in with her foot" (35). The portrait is too general and disunified to be of great value in advancing the thesis of the book.

Far better is the following chapter, "Royal Gossip," one of the most entertaining in the entire book. In an age which, according to White and to history, detested discussing matters of moral or political import, gossip about trivialities, especially the idiosyncrasies of the reigning monarch, became fashionable conversation. Concerning the five kings who presided over the age of Horace Walpole, White says: "There was something warm and ridiculous about all of them, which would have been lost except for the gossip of the age" (78). White quotes the more choice contemporary pieces of contemporary information. The Earl of Chesterfield pictured George I as a lazy, inactive, honest man who, "if he does not adorn, at least he will not stain the annals of his country" (53). George II, according to Lord Sporus Hervey, was consistently henpecked by the domineering Queen Caroline and was a touchy, comic, obstinate, small man who wanted desperately to be thought courageous and prepotent. George III, according to Fanny Burney, chased her furiously across a courtyard and madly (literally "mad"-ly) poured forth his innermost feelings and desires to her acquiescent ears.

The most colorful of the "Age of Scandal" kings, however, was George IV, a man so enamoured with his own love-making abilities that he called himself Florizel. Not England's most mature or respectable king, Florizel was known to have his physician bleed him in order to appear courtly and lovishly pale before the lady he sought and to have inflicted flesh wounds upon himself in order to play upon the sympathies of ladies not conditioned to suicidal crazes. George IV indulged himself in anything that attracted him, including shooting contests in heavily populated ballrooms. William IV, the last of the monarchs of the age, was a notorious afterdinner speaker; and he sometimes toasted as many as ninety different people individually. His passion for speaking carried into Parliament where he is known to have delivered lectures against, among other things, adultery. With kings such as these, the tone of the Age of Scandal could scarcely have been otherwise.

White's scholarship is very thorough in regard not only to people and customs but also to concepts. In *The Age of Scandal* in the chapter entitled "Bottom," White observes that "it was a word of composite meaning, which implied stability, and also what the twentieth century calls 'guts'" (80). The metaphor, derived from ships, also implies courage, coolness, and solidity. White presents, in this chapter, short vignettes about those who *had* "bottom," which was cultivated to offset the "terrors" of the age which struck persons without regard to status—gout, murder, robbery, and capital punishment for less than capital crimes. Bottom, according to Dr. Johnson, enabled one to excel as well as to remain philosophical at the moment of adversity: " 'My master whipt me very well. Without that, Sir, I should have been nothing' " (86). One of the best means of figuratively displaying one's "bottom" at times when situations did not of themselves demand it was in betting, wagering on anything at all. Rather than help a fallen human, it was more proper to bet, with an impartial friend, just how long he could remain alive. Fox-hunting, drinking, random dares to do anything foolish, and duels (White has a lengthy discourse on duels in *The Scandalmonger*) were additional means to maintain public view of one's "bottom." If the kings had their idiosyncrasies, their subjects were hard to outdo.

The Age of Scandal is a book often overly researched; frequently, it is even eccentric. Despite history's and literature's dictums against Lord Hervey,[10] he is for White one of the admirable men of the age. White presents, as well, a rather involved and barely convincing proof that a Hervey, and not Sir Robert Walpole, was really the father of Horace Walpole. In uplifting Hervey, White walks heavily across the memory of Alexander Pope, a man he obviously considered the very antithesis of the liveliness of the age he was portraying. Pope was simply too much the advocate of orderly reason to have tolerated the activities and people White finds intriguing.

In his chapter "The Mob," for example, White becomes philosophical about the comparative calm in England during the popular uprising in France in the late eighteenth century. The English aristocracy, recognizing, while loving, its own foibles, was not hypocritical; the Mob was permitted its license as well: "The license demanded by the Mob, and the good humour with which that license was conceded in England were surprising. In France, the lidded pot might eventually boil over and scald the land with blood, but, on the other side of the Channel, there was an openness between the classes which allowed the vessel to let off steam" (133). This is obviously more fanciful than philosophical; but, if the portrait White paints of the age is at all correct, the rationale might easily be supported by the zaniness of the times.

At no point in *The Age of Scandal* does any semblance of order take hold of the appearance of the portraits—the whole is a composite of madras colors. The rest of the book divides in half much the same way the first part did—individual portraits of famous, semifamous, and infamous figures interspersed with a series of anecdotes concerning foibles and customs.

These latter discussions are almost always enjoyable in themselves. The one on "Romance," for example, pictures artists and scandalmongers who can no longer resist temptation to devote themselves to the fantastic, thus detaching themselves from the *via media* stodginess of the Age of Reason. A love for the melodramatic gives birth to the Gothic novel in which Walpole, "Monk" Lewis, and others attempted to outscare one another and their reading public, for the earlier interest in the Classics had now succumbed totally to the boredom of an age which found them to be insufficiently novel. The love for Gothic tales inspired an admiration for Gothic architecture, and each of the major Gothic novelists constructed his own haunted mansion. Beckford, the author of *Vathek*, had a three-hundred-foot tower erected next to his house, but it fell within days of its completion. Walpole himself had a home called Strawberry Hill which he built at such a white heat that he had to have the tracery painted on sheets of paper which were pasted to the building and which shortly peeled. When not building, these individuals devoted their lives to collecting stories about incest and tragic love affairs which their public would eventually devour.

The portraits of individuals are not always so entertaining, though White does quite well with some of the lesser-known figures. When he attempts Johnson, however, he feebly attempts to write in ten pages what Boswell did in thousands. The Marquis de Sade suffers equally, for White concentrates almost totally on his downfall rather than on the activities of the man who, at the high points of his existence, was the terminal for every possible vice and perversion.

In addition, the drawing of George Selwyn, the necrophilist, is humorous in a sadistic sort of way. The portrayal of Carolina Matilda, in "The Injured Queen," is also well done; and her desperate attempt to avoid a preordained fate between the age of fifteen and her death at twenty-three is one of the book's most suspenseful tales. But the account of Admiral Byng in "A Perfect Tragedy" is excellent, both because he is a man who is included only because he intrigues White (whereas Johnson and de Sade *must* be included) and because the reader is likely to be encountering the before-unencountered rather than the previously endured.

Admiral Byng, having been poorly supported in a major sea encounter by the British government and having been disappointed with the winds he needed to attack in the battle, gave an order which was not transmittable by code from ship to ship. Depending upon the intelligence of his captains to realize what method of attack he was employing, Byng suffered an ignominious defeat when these same captains became panic-stricken. Thomas Pelham Holles, Duke of Newcastle, who governed England for the last seven years and who intended to keep on governing for many more, covered his own poor planning by ordering Byng to fight at the wrong time; he used the Admiral as a scapegoat, labeling him incompetent and hiring Grub Streeters to publish the fact. Despite essays in Byng's support by famous men such as Johnson and Voltaire, Byng was executed for the grievous errors of Newcastle and his captains; his life was, according to Sir Horace Mann, "a perfect tragedy" (183).

The Age of Scandal, overall, is an odd work, written by a man whose interests often outstripped his ability to cope with them. His publisher demanded books, and White produced them about whatever was on his mind—and many of his works succeed for this reason alone. However, in *The Age of Scandal*, too many loose ends and too much disorganization are apparent; indeed the work seems to be at times the first draft of a doctoral dissertation. The volume is repetitious, for the same vignette is often used in connection with different topics. The book, in short, is the raw product of a man who, for a few years of his life, wished to be a scholar. This statement is not meant to imply that the book is not readable—often it is enjoyable and humorous, as almost everything White wrote at one point or another ultimately is. In addition to the several individual pieces recommended above, White has collected fourteen fine illustrations of people and events from the "Age of Scandals"; he has provided at the back of the book very fine notes to explain them. Although the "Age of Scandal" was never exactly defined before White's unsuccessful attempt to define it, no doubt exists that the period was one of mischievousness, rakishness, and indeed of bloodthirstiness and sadism which set the tone, it seems, for the entire social structure from the king to the mob. In the sequel, entitled *The Scandalmonger*, White provides more examples of the same.

IV The Scandalmonger

The Scandalmonger[11] follows virtually the same format as its predecessor, *The Age of Scandal*. Its quality, while again often entertaining, is not quite so high; for we constantly have the impression of an overflow of research, of more diffuseness of leftovers than the first conveyed; in short, we find more questionably relevant items in this volume than in the first. The personal portraits are of about the same quality as those of the first volume, but those of known figures are again not quite so good as those focusing upon lesser-knowns. Indeed, the two best portrayals are those of Lord Camelford and of Beau Brummel.

Sylvia Warner considers the Camelford portrait to be a serious flaw of the book; for, while most of the others "are sensible as well as entertaining," an "exception occurs in the second volume where, at the opening of 'A Struggle of Sentiment,' White's self-identification with Lord Camelford is like a spurt of blood."[12] The self-identification is certainly present; and, had it come within the structure of a novel, it would have been detrimental. But White, in writing two books about the same era, certainly feels an affinity for an age he considers far more exciting than his own; and, in the portrait of Camelford, White has found the reason why he does so—the "Age of Scandal" reserved a place for persons such as he. Camelford is a superman who endeavors to outdo his fellowman in everything, and we might connect this character with the sadness-learning statement in *The Sword in the Stone*.[13] About supermen in general and Camelford in particular, and more particularly about himself, White remarks in *The Scandalmonger*:

> The soul of the superman is probably an unhappy one. He believes himself to be a coward at heart, and so, to conceal this, he is forced to prodigies of useless valour. He believes himself to be inferior to his companions; therefore he must force himself to beat them at everything. He detests his own character, so he must seek to make others love it. He is perhaps deeply sincere, with high romantic ideals, self-critical, intelligent, and of a sensitive nature. Hating cruelty for sentimental reasons, he observes that he himself is cruel. What he is, he despises; what he is not, he seeks to be.
>
> Camelford was an example of these paradoxes. . . . Believing himself to be a coward, and that most other people were not cowards, he had to become the second-best pistol-shot in the kingdom, and one of the most dreaded of its duellists. He was forced to be terrible to those who opposed him, while being generous to a fault with those who accepted his leadership. Humble enough to throw away any advantages in his profession—as a naval officer—which came to him by birth or by influence, his satanic pride led him to fight, tooth and nail, for any advantages which he thought he had truly earned. Capable as an officer, and peremptory with his superiors, his high ambition for deserved success was doomed to achieve nothing. Professing infidelity, he made romantic and touching plans for the disposal of his corpse. (25–26)[14]

Except for certain specific details it is difficult to tell how much of this character is Camelford's and how much of it is White's own character and his own catharsis.

The remainder of the Camelford portrait is a semi-Dostoevskian picture of a superman who turned thug. Finally, after fabricating the circumstances for his change to satisfy his own ego, Camelford dies in a duel with the kingdom's best shot. White quotes Farington's sympathetic obituary: "That He possessed such abilities that could He have survived 10 years longer till the heat of Youth shd. have passed away & the mind have settled, *He would have been the first Man of the age*" (32).

The Scandalmonger's penultimate chapter, "The Butterfly," is a humorous rendition of the life of Beau Brummel and is one of the most memorable parts of the book. Complete with a picture which displays Brummel in all his prissiness, White recounts the several hours (literally) that the butterfly spent each day in completing his toilet. Having finally dressed and powdered himself, he would daily set forth about the town to be "as rude to everybody as could be" (198)—one of this effeminate creature's methods to prove his "bottom," which he inflicted upon high and low alike. He is known, after having dined with the future king of England, to have said, in fact " 'Wales, . . . ring the bell' " (200). To match and sharpen his insolence, his trademarks were his famous bow (which, according to White, was necessitated by his tight cravat) and his jeweled snuffboxes, which he could open, use, and close with one hand. Others often could not resist challenging him to a duel, a challenge the physically incapable Brummel invariably insulted them out of. His later life, however, was spent in a poorhouse (another of his means to "bottom" was gambling); and his body had become so corpulent and so slobbish that someone to care for him could not even be hired.

White also relates tales about Fanny Burney, the Prince of Palagonia, Richard Sheridan, and Queen Victoria, but none of these is quite so memorable. We wonder, in fact, that Victoria should be included as part of the Age, but White justifies her presence by stating that both she and the Age combine the sublime with the ridiculous. One other portrait which is quite well done, perhaps the most poignant piece in either volume, is that of a seaman named John Nichol who, while transporting female convicts to the South Seas, falls in love with one and vows to jump ship on the return trip in order to spend the rest of his life with her. Upon returning to the island after four years of trying to do so he is unable to find her and spends the rest of his life penniless in his futile search.

Like *The Age of Scandal*, this work also contains several topical presentations, the best of which is the opening chapter about duels, one which is bloody and comic concurrently. The first vignette, which provides a memorable opening, concerns a duel (people of the age duelled at the drop of a hat) over a hat between two Frenchmen, Bazanez and Lagarde:

> They set out . . . on the instant. Lagarde came down with a vigorous cut on the head of Bazanez, but the frontal bone was so hard that it turned off the weapon. The second cut, however, went in, and Lagarde said, "That's for the hat." "This is for the feather," he added, with another thrust. "And this is for the tassel," a third time he said by way of conclusion. Bazanez lost a great deal of blood, but was not done for yet. He made an extreme effort, rushed upon his op-

ponent, and got him down. In this position he drove his poignard repeatedly in a line between his neck and shoulder, saying, "I am giving you a scarf to wear with the hat." He gave him fourteen stabs from the neck to the navel. At each stab Bazanez exclaimed, "Beg for your life." "No, no!" said Lagarde, "not yet, my dear fellow"; and hacked about as he was in every part of his body, he bit off the chin of his slaughterer, and smashed the back of his head with the pommel of his sword. This put an end to the conflict. (9–10)

Both men, surprisingly enough, lived. Despite a liberal sprinkling of gore, however, the treatment of the duel is almost flippant, by White and by the Age. These spontaneous brawls and haggles soon became very well-organized events. More comical than the rules and manners were the eccentricities of the duelists themselves: "Men began to meet in gravel pits, in coaches, in the dark. In 1808, an enterprising couple fought in two balloons. By 1843, a meeting had taken place with billiard balls. The balls had to be thrown at each other's head by hand, and the combatants tossed a coin for the first shy, which proved fatal. The famous duelist Stackpole, on being shot dead by a person called Cecil, observed as he fell: 'By George, I've missed him!'" (20).

White, who even researched the casualty statistics, found that only one in five duelists died; and, in at least half of the duels fought during the "Age of Scandal," not a drop of blood was spilled. If duelling should seem half-witted and barbaric to the twentieth-century reader, White counters such an impression with a statement highly reminiscent of the Arthurian tetralogy: "We fight wars about the imaginary lines called frontiers, believing war to be capable of justice and sacrificing the lives of young people by tens of millions, against their will. We have abolished the duel, which used to kill ten men a year in the third George's reign, and we are proud of this great step in civilization, like a dog with two tails" (21). Duels, to White, are not a sign of barbarism—they keep society polite, lest the "impolite" be forced to endure the likes of this one.

In the chapter "Various Comforters" White portrays the era's interest in dogs, an interest which often led people to value the life of the canine more than that of the human being. Several of the chapters which follow are of limited interest. While "Dry Blood and Distant Thunder," an essay on man's inhumanity to man, holds attention through sheer shock value, chapters such as "Backwaters," an examination of small towns where not much happened, and "A Private Paestum," an evaluation of palace behavior, smack of leftover notes which just had to be included. The chapter entitled "Eccentrics," a title which sounds universally redundant in a book about the "Age of Scandal," provides some of the book's most humorous accounts. Especially memorable are the Duke of Queensbury—an old chap who sat on his balcony to watch, through a spyglass, the young damsels go down the street, but all the time he had a fast horse stationed nearby so he could run down the ones he found appealing—and the Chevalier d'Eon, notorious about town as a hermaphrodite.

"Bribery and Corruption" (on the cost of being elected to a public office) is too burdened with statistics to be enjoyable or memorable reading. "Fire! Fire!," like many of these little essays, is too small to tell much about anything; but this one about the universal fear of being burned to death in one's sleep does conclude with a humorous anecdote about the poet Thomas Gray and some undergraduates at a neighboring university.

After a very short chapter, too short to be informative, about Mary Shelley's *Frankenstein* (according to White, Dr. Frankenstein was a bore, a combination of Byron and Percy Bysshe), we find near the end of the volume a chapter entitled "Scandal"—the chapter, in fact, that those who wonder about the presence of the same word in the titles of both volumes have been waiting for. This essay is actually a group of two dozen unconnected vignettes which demonstrate the scandalous tittle-tattle that the Age loved to spread and which yields White "some slight excuse for dubbing theirs the Age of Scandal" (175). Some of these are amusing; most, however, are not.

The Scandalmonger enjoys the same assets and suffers from the same defects that characterize *The Age of Scandal.* Basically humorous and informative, the second book is also disjointed and lacking a thesis. It is everything an interested devotee could discover about the eccentricity and the dash of one of history's most eccentric and dashing ages. With the Lord Camelford portrait and little asides here and there about war, dogs, human relationships, and the like, we get a bit, at least, of an insight into White the man. And this man, as his life and his last paragraph in this volume demonstrate, is not the thoroughgoing humanist or liberal that most men of letters in the twentieth century like to think they are. To quote this conclusion is to demonstrate White's thinking in the early 1950's and to cite the reasons that the Age of Scandal so greatly attracted him:

> Well, the road is clear now and they are all safely past. All the fantastic kings and noblemen of the age which we have been discussing have given way before the demonstrably false proposition of Washington that all men are born equal. They are not. Dr. Johnson was born with scrofula, while Sixteen-string Jack the highwayman was born with a perfect body; Selwyn was born a fool, while Porson came into the world with the brain of a great scholar. I for one am sorry to see the old distinctions go. I would rather have lived at a time when the private enterprise of a great Duke could produce the lovely palace of Stowe with all its graces, rather than now, when an omnipotent proletariat can rear a block of offices to house the redundant inspectors and the forms in triplicate of the T.U.C. [Trades Union Congress]. (253)

V The Goshawk

The Goshawk is, in almost every way, a beautiful book. Like *America at Last*, it is the journal of a vital man at the peak of his vitality. It is, despite the scorn expressed for the Romantics in the two "Scandal" books, the picture of a man whose very soul, by means of his firm and loving attempts to know one creature perfectly, has become one with the universe: "... Gos was one, as I was one ... so insignificant as to be significant, so transitory as to be eternal, so finite as to be infinite and a part of the Becoming. How should we feel fear or impatience, being so large and small? Rouse, Gos, I besought him, warble and preen yourself: sit, austringer, on God's fist quietly as Gos on yours" (60–61).[15]

The Goshawk is actually about two different birds which White owned successively between 1936 and 1938. The major part of the volume deals with the antiquated training of the first one, Gos by name, which White purchased in Shropshire on July 29, 1936. After six weeks of patient training and meticulous journal-keeping, Gos escaped in mid-September because of White's carelessness; and the bird, unused to fending for itself, surely died soon after. The second, named Cully, was acquired in mid-April of the following year, but she too died at Easter a year later by hanging herself—again because of White's carelessness—in some strawberry netting in a barn. Cully's death, however, is not part of *The Goshawk*.

The daybook which he wrote during the coaching of Gos was initially intended to be the year's debt-reliever for White, but the unfinished work lay dormant for twelve years, probably because of his confusion created by Gos's escape and the retraining of the second hawk. After the manuscript was discovered in March, 1949, by Wren Howard of Cape under a seat cushion at Alderney, Howard read it in bed that night and then demanded that White let him publish it. White, embarrassed for reasons we will soon examine, refused. When Garnett later persuaded him that it was the finest thing he had yet written, White reluctantly let him publish it.[16] White, however, insisted that he be allowed to attach the postscript which many, myself included, feel detracts seriously from an otherwise pure and unpretentious piece of work. Once again, the publication came about fifteen years after the writing.

The book is structured in three parts plus an after-thought, the Postscript. Part I, the longest, is divided into five chapters which describe the six-week companionship between the author and Gos during which time the five steps to the kill are painstakingly worked out between man and beast, only, when on the brink of success, to have the bird escape. Part II covers the despair of White himself, plus two searches—one for Gos and, later, one for a new hawk. Part III is a brief account of a trained hawk, now Cully, that makes its first kill. The Postscript is an unnecessarily shame-faced estimate of how the training process *should have* been carried out.

The book was never intended to be a manual; but, while not the essential matter, the method of manning a hawk does constitute much of the work's intrigue. The extent of White's knowledge of falconry at the outset of his endeavors was garnered from three out-dated books on the subject—Gilbert Blaine's, one from the Badminton Library, and White's "bible" *Treatise of Hawks and Hawking* that was written by Bert in 1619. From the last work he learned that there were very important milestones to be watched for in manning a hawk: "The moment when the hawk first ate, the moment when it gave into its master after the watch, the moment when it flew to his fist, the moment when it flew to him the distance of a hundred yards, and the moment when it made its kill" (55).

Because the fledgling austringer had a food supply prepared and because the bird was enormously hungry when it arrived, the first step was too easily accomplished (later White suffered from the lethargy of an overfed bird). The second, that of "watching," required two lengthy and laborious sessions to complete. Watching, White's directions said, was the fairest way to accustom a hawk to depending upon its master for absolutely everything since any torture the bird had to endure the man also suffered. Essentially, watching involved keeping the bird (and the falconer) awake with assorted methods for three solid days, in order to make the bird come to sit on the master's hand, if for no other reason than being allowed to go to sleep finally. During this time, however, the weary falconer had to be careful to show neither temper nor irritation because goshawks, being sensitive birds, have a proclivity for choosing to die if the world seems too harsh. In short, White's problem was to teach the hawk, gently, in two months what the bird could have acquired naturally in two days of freedom.

White, who carefully followed the directions on watching, hardly closed his eyes for three days. Feeling like an executioner the entire time, he began to see minute signs of success, even in counting the diminishing number of bates (impatient wing beating) the bird manifested each hour. In fact, sometime during this period White decided to write his book because he felt the steps to improvement were so small but crucial that they required documentation. Finally the end of the long three days came:

When Gos finally gave in, the conquest was a visible one. Sitting on the fist, his head drooped, and his wings mantled. No longer firm and spruce at the shoulders, they hung down on either side of the body, humbly resting their forward edges against the supporting arm. The eyelids irresistibly rose up over the capitulated eyes, the head nodded for sleep which his master, as tired as he was, was forced by a gentle movement to deny him. Between the two protagonists a link had been established, of pity on the one side and confidence on the other. We had waited patiently for seventy-two hours for this moment; the moment at which the hawk, co-erced by no cruelty of mine but only by the desire for sleep (which he did not connect with me), could first say with confidence: "I am so sleepy that I will trust this glove as a perch to sleep on, even though you stroke me, even though you have no wings and a beak of pliable gristle." (31–32)

One of the most discouraging things about manning his hawk was to White the ease of regression. After allowing the hawk to go to sleep, he discovered it had retreated a long way toward wildness with just a little rest. In fact, regression was evident every morning—one step forward and two steps backward seemed to be the formula for "progress" despite the more than twelve hours a day that he devoted to the bird. A day off, of course, was out of the question. At times the pressure showed signs of cracking both the trainer and the hawk—"rage was contagious between unconscious hearts" (41). The hawk, on these occasions, bated furiously; but, White found, it performed much better after venting its anger. This battle of wits continued for nearly a month.

During this period White noticed "hunger traces," a weakening of the bird's tail feathers which decreased efficient flight. To correct this weakness, the versatile amateur austringer "imped" them—cut off the old feathers at the weak spot and attached a moulted feather with a triangular needle. Despite the lack of efficiency he demonstrated in other areas of the training, especially in feeding the bird too generously, he seems to have been competent in this endeavor.

After what seemed a longer period of time than it actually was, White felt ready to take the hawk to the outside world to accustom it to the noises amidst which it would have to work. But Gos's poor reaction to cars, people, and the noises of harvest, coupled with an overall slowdown in its progress (due to being overfed), necessitated, in White's mind, the accomplishing of a second watch. Three more days—long ones—followed during which White danced to swing music and quoted Shakespeare to the bird in a valiant effort to keep awake. Much more able to discipline his own affection for the animal, White became a firmer master after this episode; he fed the animal only when it had performed correctly and disciplined it to respond to a whistled hymn, "The Lord is My Shepherd."

After this training came the more practical steps of increasing the leash daily to make the bird fly farther for his food. One of the book's most graphic moments occurs a few days before the ultimate one-hundred-yard test, where White was holding the long creance in one hand, a piece of meat in the other:

> His wings beat with a measured purpose, the two eyes of his low-held head fixed me with a ghoulish concentration: but like headlamps, like the forward-fixed eyes of a rower through the air who knew his quay. . . . Too menacingly he flew, not toward the at-right-angles-held-out beef, but directly toward my face. At five paces nerve broke. I ducked, still holding the beef at the stretch of my arm, and stayed coweringly for two beats of my heart. . . . Before I could see where he had gone, while I was still bunching together for the strike, Gos slewed off on a misstoop, flew to the nearest tree of the riding, missed his grip of it because the creance caught him short (very luckily), hung inverted for a moment, dropped into the hedge. (106)

Despite his resolve not to break on the second strike, White cringed again, though Gos successfully snagged the meat and settled on his shoulder. Two days later, despite many hindrances, the bird flew the entire one-hundred-yard distance.

The rest of the first section evinces a tone of relief and cock-sureness on White's part. In retrospect, it all seemed easier than it was supposed to be. Amid allowing the bird more and more freedom and trying to make it fly fast as well as straight, the goshawk—because the string holding him in the barn was cheap and had broken twice before and because, as Warner says, White was often more thrifty than prudent with his money—escaped. Though the hawkless austringer observed Gos, flying freely with other birds for a good week afterwards, it was never recaptured. The brokenhearted author tried to console himself that the bird was better off with its freedom; he later, in the Postscript, admits that Gos almost assuredly died soon after, for he had never been taught how to seek his own food.

Part II is concerned mainly with White's search for Gos in the thickets, his tying food to his perches "like the parents of Peter Pan" (143), and his devising ingenious new traps to capture a "passage hawk" during the hawks' fall migration. When he succeeds at none of these, he eventually purchases another hawk, Cully, from the German falconer who had originally captured Gos. Though the reader wishes Gos and not Cully was making the kill which brings the book to a close (after all, Cully was being trained only between pages 194 and 195), the final kill is exciting and heartwarming. Cully, from the time White bought her, had very poor tail feathering—her flight was never graceful or efficient. The easiest game escaped her, frustrating both herself and her kind and tolerant master. Her first kill finally came on a Tuesday in the midsummer of 1937. White deliberately sought easy game for her, knowing that her morale was low. But still, both on account of the hawk's poor physical condition and on account of White's inexperienced flying of her, they experienced twelve failures on this particular morning. But then Cully, battling furiously, ungracefully, and inefficiently, killed a rabbit hiding in the grass—but she *still* killed it. Much of her success was due to the compassionate heart of her austringer who, knowing his hawk would never be a champion, all but pushed the animal in her path and all but blocked it when it ran. But the feat was at long last accomplished, and White went home to a bottle of champagne, Cully to a tasty rabbit.

But, as White admits in the unnecessary Postscript, he did it all wrong. Falconry, contrary to his suspicions, was a living art which he had learned with seventeenth-century techniques: "It was not . . . dead . . . , something that ended in 1619, but a growing and progressing skill which had developed into something quite different by 1950, and which will continue to develop" (205). In a few subsequent paragraphs, he outlines generally what he had done wrong and the useless hours he had invested when quicker ways of training had long ago been developed.

Since much of the book's zest and charm derives from the fact that White was an amateur, an innocent, the Postscript can only detract and should, I feel, be disregarded as much as possible. White, a man with great interest in medieval and Renaissance culture, tried to return to the hawking those eras knew. Better ways are often found through such an approach, but White overlooks this factor in trying to cover his embarrassment before the knowing falconers he is afraid will read his book. His diagrams, some fourteen of them, both clarify for the uninitiated reader exactly what he is talking about and demonstrate the interest and cleverness of a devotee who almost daily developed new and more efficient traps and perches from those with which he was initially acquainted. These, while not modern, are tremendously interesting; and they clarify in a way that other books on the subject, Turberville's say, do not.

We remarked earlier[17] that one of the most satisfying aspects of this book is White's own particular brand of Romanticism, but he would have cringed at the term itself. Perhaps this metaphysical experience was aided by his outmoded approach. White, who continually makes reference to the history of falconry, often places himself timelessly within the tradition he had so recently entered. He reflects at one point that it is fine to be part of a no-longer-dominant civilization and to have the time and experience to indulge in something so seemingly unnecessary as hawking. At another he takes Gos to the ruins of a medieval chapel, and the aura of timelessness is all the more evident as White considers himself free of rising Fascism while he is practicing a medievally timeless sport in a medievally atemporal setting.

But a transcendence of time is only one aspect of the "romanticism," for other characteristics are more essential in pinpointing just exactly what White accomplishes in a book so seemingly limited in interest. Though the purposes and the circumstances are different, the book is at least reminiscently Thoreauvian. White, in 1936–37, was a man anxious to escape the world of capital, the rumors of Hitler, the inconsistencies of human beings. By escaping from man and the universe, he comes to know the human and universal spirits. His dictum for nature and against man *qua* man is evident from the opening page. The following passage, one of the book's most beautiful and most memorable, delineates the arrival of Gos at White's home in Stowe Ridings:

> Imagine what his life had been till then. When he was an infant, still unable to fly and untidy with bits of fluff, still that kind of mottled, motive and gaping toad which confronts when we look into birds' nest in May: when, moreover, he was a citizen of Germany, so far away: a glaring man had come to his mother's nest with a basket like this one, and had stuffed him in. He had never seen a human being, never been confined in such a box, which smelled of

darkness and manufacture and the stink of man. It must have been like death—the thing which we can never know beforehand—as, with clumsy talons groping for an unnatural foothold, his fledgling consciousness was hunched and bundled in the oblong alien surroundingness. The guttural voices, the unbirdlike den he was taken to, the scaly hands which bound him, the second basket, the smell and noise of the motor car, the unbearable, measured clamour of the aircraft which bounced those skidding talons on the untrustworthy woven floor all the way to England: heat, fear, noise, hunger, the reverse of nature; with these to stomach, terrified, but still nobly and madly defiant, the eyas goshawk had arrived at my small cottage in his accursed basket. . . . He was born to fly, sloping sideways, free among the verdure of that Teutonic upland, to murder with his fierce feet and to consume with that curved Persian beak, who now hopped up and down in the clothes basket with a kind of imperious precocity, the impatience of a spoiled but noble heir apparent to the Holy Roman Empire. (11–12)

To compensate the bird for what he has lost, White tacitly resolves to treat the bird as "naturally" as he can; and this resolve requires that he think "naturally" at all times. Suddenly the man and bird begin to reciprocate: "Part of the joy was that now, for the first time in my life, I was absolutely free. Even if I only had a hundred pounds, I had no master, no property, no fetters. I could eat, sleep, rise, stay, go as I liked. I was freer than the archbishop of Canterbury, who no doubt had his fixed times and seasons. I was free as a hawk" (39).

If White resembles Thoreau here, he later speaks like Wordsworth in "Tintern Abbey" and in one of the earlier books of "The Prelude":

It [Life] thundered in far surf on distant breakers, or, like a buried dynamo, droned out its power: . . . As I walked home in the evening it was melted together: the public house five miles away, where I had arrived long before anybody woke up [walking with Gos]: the hawk chastened and feeding well, even in the bar parlour among curious men: . . . the beer slow and swelling in the throat: the warm hearts: the hard body wending its indirect courses: the meadowsweet dead: the red moon perceptibly rising, which I had seen to sink as a yellow one at dawn. (52–53)

In short, White, through his experiences with Gos, short-lived though they were, had become a "Living Soul"[18]—a feeling he was probably not to enjoy again until his trip to America in 1963. His earlier rejection of man assumes, later in the book, Shelleyan proportions of sympathy: "It [war] did not matter, so long as man survived. If after the battle this race could be left mature, nothing would have been lost. Let the Empire and the glory pass away with a Wagnerian crash, so long as the voice and the zither still mentioned their patient melody on the unburdened air. A few peaks of human achievement would survive: peaks of patience and conquest by culture: peaks of maturity in education" (72).

As in almost all of White's books of the 1930's and early 1940's,[19] there is continual reference to war. The one cited above sounds somewhat more liberal than one with which we are familiar from *The Once and Future King*, the "Scandal" books, and *The Elephant and the Kangaroo*; but many of the others duplicate the tone of these books. Early in the book he counters his friends' complaints that he devotes his talents to teaching birds to kill rabbits with the argument that men of greater ability seemed in these days to devote their effort to the elimination of whole portions of the human race. In another instance, he rationalizes to himself that falconry is a useful skill since the World War (two years away) would reduce man to savagery and since he would, once again, have to hunt for his own sustenance. His most summational and most personal statement comes midway: "It [war] was pointless, cruel, wasteful, and to the lonely individual terrible" (71). As in almost all his books, White never is able to stick solely to his subject—reflections must always creep in. In this book they succeed, for it is written by a man who is somehow one with a universal spirit which transcends and is obliged to encompass all.

It should not be thought, however, that *The Goshawk* is a book only for sporting or philosophical minds, for it is not. A story of persistent human endeavor, it is relevant to all and also consistently entertaining. Despite the disappointments which naturally appear every few pages, the comic side of life is often in evidence: "Providence was very fair on the whole, only at present it delighted to jog me" (182); and these "jogs" are varied. To keep himself awake, he had to recite to Gos hawking passages from Shakespeare. In moments of frustration, he swung

Tarzan-like through the rafters of the barn, chasing the frightened hawk to the barn's farthest corners. Often the hawk itself is the comic figure, as when it sits amidst its plumes in a puddle of water. Often the onlookers have curious reactions to what the eccentric young man was doing, as when White took Gos out for his first long flight: "His bates at the people were less annoying than the people's reaction to him. Nervous mothers wheeled their children's perambulators to the opposite pavements, exclaiming women stepped out on the road in front of motors, rather than pass us within a yard, while troops of children followed us about" (101).

But the comedy is often tragi-comedy. Take, for example, the picture of White, now hawkless because of his carelessness with Gos, hiding Lazurus-like under a layer of sod. Though he had hoped to catch either Gos or a new hawk, all he caught was a cold from lying twelve hours in a soaking rain. At another point, having invented an ingenious trap, he goes home for several hours, hoping to find the trap sprung when he returns; but he finds that well-meaning but less-experienced friends have disassembled his trap and built a new, not-so-efficient one in its place.

The Goshawk is, to me, one of White's richest books, one which lacks readers because of its seemingly limited subject. White, never a great lover of mankind, is almost totally separated from it as he deals with the creatures of nature that he loves. Through his experience with them, he gains much greater insights into the method and reason for living—subjects which were of lifelong concern to him. This work is, in every way, a minor classic.

CHAPTER 6

The Last Ten Years

I The Book of Beasts

IT is natural, I think, for a man of White's intellect and great love of knowledge and learning things, for whatever reason this love was nurtured and preserved, to want, at some point in his life, to be a scholar.[1] *The Bestiary: A Book of Beasts* is the product of such a desire: "The first thing to tell you is that I am in the seventh heaven with my Bestiary, etc. I was always intended to be a scholar—thwarted by buggers like you—and now I am being one at last, off my own bat. My preface to my Bestiary is going to put Sir James Frazer in the ice box and will quote from 43 authorities beginning with the letter A alone."[2]

As White confesses, his Latin was rusty when he ambitiously began his bestiary on December 21, 1938. At that time, his plan was to translate a page a day and to complete the project within a year; but the work was not completed and published until 1954. Many reasons other than his slow progress in Latin caused the fifteen-year delay; for White, while working on many of his books, was subject to the procrastination that supposedly besets most authors. Moreover, World War II occurred, a time, as we have seen already, when books were difficult to publish in England and when, White thought, there were more constructive things to write than medieval bestiaries. It was, in fact, not until October, 1943, after having mollified his agonizing doubts about war and human destiny, that the first word was ever translated. Before making much progress, he was overcome by Brownie's death; and the work again lay dormant for many months.

By April, 1945, however, it was half-completed; but his enthusiasm for it was causing him to spend more time and money in the research than he had originally planned. Another difficulty which caused the endeavor to extend nine more years was his inability, as many of his books show, to attach himself to one project at a time. Instead of finishing *The Bestiary,* he contemporaneously wrote *The Age of Scandal* and *The Scandalmonger.* The book finally appeared in 1954 and received a warm reception by students but a frigid rejection from critics. White was enormously disappointed and bitter.

The bestiary itself, generally known as the Roxburghe Bestiary, is one from the twelfth century, which is preserved in the Cambridge University Library and, in 1928, was edited for the Roxburghe Club by Dr. M. R. James. White's version is far more than a translation, for in it he preserved one hundred twenty-five illustrations from the original manuscript. The clarity these provide to the often overly disguised descriptions in the text is incalculable. White follows the translation with an appendix containing a simplified version of the items usually found in such scholarly texts of manuscripts as the *Anglo-Saxon Poetic Record* of George Philip Krapp and Elliott Van Kirk Dobbie.

White, who is primarily interested in making the bestiary appeal to the common reader, nonetheless tries to be scholarly and entertaining at the same time. Particularly interesting is his concise analysis of the bestiary tradition, beginning with the *Physiologus* of prebestiary times, which was a popular animal picture book for many centuries. He describes how the bestiary grew out of the *Physiologus* and how individual bestiaries grew in size every time a new traveler came through a certain bestiary-writing area with new tales of strange beasts. Later Marco Polo and Sir John Mandeville began to add credibility by verifying the existence of some beasts and by expressing public doubt about some of the more fantastic animals that bestiaries had hitherto claimed existed. In the seventeenth century, as White indicates, Sir Thomas Browne, in subjecting the bestiary tradition to rational analysis, wrote the *Pseudodoxia Epidemica,* the first book of modern biology. White is thus continually emphatic about the more-than-fairy-tale importance of the bestiary.

For White (and, he hopes, for his reader) the bestiary is an extremely enjoyable mode of learning; for, once the fairy tale syndrome is negated, the real intelligence and the perspicacity of the art are wonderfully apparent. He scorns those who ridicule such strange animals as, say, the Cameleopard. Could there not be such an animal that an uninitiated observer would be able to name only by combining the names of more familiar beasts? Could the Cameleopard really be a giraffe? Deciphering and rendering credible what seems on the surface fantastic, are, for White, the educational enjoyment of a bestiary.

After a short section about how medieval books in general and bestiaries in particular were written, White provides a short but interesting discussion of the symbolic value of bestiaries. Supernatural truths were often "clarified" for the medieval Christian by associating Christ with, for instance, an elephant. Almost all bestiaries were moralistic in tone, for they were true to the medieval concept of *sapientia* (all wisdom and knowledge were irrelevant if not directed toward the salvation of the immortal soul).[3] Some were parabolic, some were moral fables, and many were strictly platonic insights into the nature and perfection of God. This aspect, for White, is probably the most significant: the bestiary, like all literature, is a guide to the civilizing principles of a society.

The Appendix concludes with a shorter-than-usual description of the translator's liberties (any concession to making the finished product more enjoyable was taken) and with a bibliography of over two hundred scholarly entries which demonstrate better than anything else one major reason why the final product required fifteen years to complete—the translator became fantastically interested in his material and did not limit himself only to the minutiae that could cleverly be passed on to his reader.

As for the translated bestiary itself, we need to examine a typical portrait of an animal and to notice both the writer's technique (which so interested White) and the translator's rendition. The opening portrait is of the Lion, which the author (not White) calls, despite the fantastic animals of the twelfth century, the "mightiest of beasts" (7).[4] The author proceeds to furnish general information about the Lion—physical constitution, things it is afraid of, the root of its name, and so forth—while attempting to be as objective as possible about facts which have no allegorical or didactic significance. When the author arrives at the Lion's three principal characteristics, his objectivity gives way to the moralisms. The first characteristic is the lion's habit of going to the top of a mountain and, if he finds he is being pursued there by hunters, covering his trail by dragging his brushlike tail in the dust. The original composer of this entry cannot resist this observation: "It was in this way that our Saviour . . . once hid the spoor of his love in the high places, until, being sent by the Father, he came down into the womb of the Virgin Mary and saved the human race which had perished" (8).

The second characteristic is the animal's open-eyed sleeping, about which the bestiariest remarks: "In this very way, our Lord also, while sleeping in the body was buried after being crucified—yet his Godhead was awake. As it is said in the *Song of Songs*, 'I am asleep and my heart is awake,' or, in the Psalm, 'Behold he that keepeth Israel shall neither slumber nor sleep' " (8). The third characteristic is that the lioness brings forth her new cubs dead and maintains them so for three days until the Father, appearing on the third day, breathes upon them (growls?) and brings them to life. The moralist observes: "Just so did the Father Omnipotent raise Our Lord Jesus Christ from the dead on the third day. Quoth Jacob: 'He shall sleep like a lion, and the lion's whelp shall be raised' " (8–9).

Not content to stop with only three similarities, the original author (following tradition) provides one sharp distinction for the spiritual benefit of all: the lion does not get angry unless he is wounded; but this behavior is unsatisfactory for a Christian because Christ instructed man not to get angry even with the guilty. The morality and spirituality of the bestiary tradition often seem strained, often appear more based upon superstition than fact. However, as Augustine himself points out, what is demonstrated is important (the moral lesson involved), not the biological or strictly logical credibility of the facts themselves. *Sapientia* (wisdom) always rules over *scientia* (knowledge). The second half of the portrait is again a series of random facts and unapplied information about the lion's habits, and it is presented more for information than for any more important purpose.

This general approach of the bestiary tradition is found in

each of the portraits, but White's contributions have not yet been considered. Though he makes a concerted effort throughout not to be scholarly in the obtrusive sense, White can never permit himself to sacrifice precision. Thus, his translation is first of all carried out in a smooth prose which avoids the natural stumblings of the amateur *vis à vis* pony writer. He maintains the modern idiom: in literal Latin, the lion wanders "without severe concern," but in White's version he is "fancy free." This usage is obviously for the reader's benefit, but White is often not content to let the idiom have full play. In trying, for example, to come to grips with the tradition's handling of the word "beast," he feels compelled to show the knowledgeable reader the Latin meanings that are involved: "They are called Beasts because of the violence with which they rage, and are known as "wild" (*ferus*) because they are accustomed to freedom by nature and are governed (*ferantur*) by their own wishes" (7).

White often inserts material that helps in the symbolic interpretation of a passage as well as with the literal one. When the bestiariest enters upon the seemingly far-fetched comparison of Christ with the Lion, White inserts reference to "the Spiritual Lion of the Tribe of Judah" in parentheses into the text itself. Often when longer, interesting-though-not-immediately-relevant matters arise, he constructs long footnotes which widen the scope of apparently limited material. For instance, the lion will not attack a prostrate adversary; and White elaborates in a note:

> Dr. Johnson's Mrs. Thrale narrated an interesting anecdote about one of her ancestors (Hayward, ii, 8) without being aware that it derived from the bestiariests. The ancestor was a Sir Henry de Salusbury, who bore "the Bavarian lion" in his shield. An opponent whom he had conquered in the battle prostrated himself before Sir Henry, observing: *Sat est prostrasse leoni.* Charmed by this tactful and apposite quotation, which shows that bestiaries must have been familiar to both combatants, Sir Henry spared his suppliant: and must have repeated the story rather frequently afterwards, to have impressed it upon the family mind to a generation so distant as that of Mrs. Thrale. (9)

Some of the material included in the parenthetical explanations and in the footnotes was garnered by White from the James edition, but the greater part of it came, once again, from the works listed in the enormous bibliography at the end of his text.

The important aspect of White's contribution is, however, that the reader is enjoying himself with each description and is putting together the pieces free of the hindrances of sluggish rhetoric, obscure allusions, distant theology, and a feeling of extreme barbarity in the material he is reading. White's greatest contribution is that, generally, he makes the book real and relevant.

It is difficult to discuss the *Book of Beasts* in a study such as this one; for, despite the considerable amount White did for an old book hitherto hardly accessible, the great bulk of the bestiary belongs to an unknown writer who is not our present concern. Yet this anonymous author, who is really only a figurehead for an important tradition, obviously had great influence upon White's masterwork; for the concepts of *caritas* and *cupiditas, sapientia* and *scientia*—concepts so important for an accurate reading of *The Once and Future King*—are insistently evident throughout his bestiary. White probably did not learn of these for the first time through the Roxburghe Bestiary, but he must certainly have been aided by the lucidity of their presentation in it. In this bestiary, the Monkey is chided because he has no tail: "he has a head, but no scripture" (34). In medieval life, White became certain, a man without a similar allegorical tail was no man; for, if he did not love and learn (*caritas* and *sapientia*) for the greater glory of God, he was actually not worth considering. In Lancelot and Arthur, White developed this demanding dichotomy to its utmost limits.

II The Master

The Master is, in every way, one of White's poorest books. White's greatest fault as a novelist is his inability to attempt one thing in a book rather than several discordant things. Although published in 1957, the story and its central character were first conceived in 1941 soon after the fifth book of the Arthurian series, "The Book of Merlyn," was declined by the publishers. Merlyn was thinly disguised in the character of Alpha (as recorded in White's notebooks), a wise man of one hundred thirty-two years who recognized the survival of the fittest approach to life three years before Darwin. When *The Master* (Alpha renamed) was finally written sixteen years later, the author had converted his original idea of a novel of one man's philosophical speculations into an adventure story for young readers. The book goes awry, essentially, because it ends by being half of each.

The Master is dedicated to Robert Louis Stevenson because White considered this book his own *Treasure Island,* the type of story he would have liked to have read as a boy. The tale is about eleven-year-old twins, Nicky and Judy, who, at the opening of the book, are exploring with relatives and friends the tiny island of Rockall in the north Atlantic. Apparently barren, the huge rock houses a fantastic scientific experiment which, if successful, will put the entire world under the control of one unknown man, the Master. When the twins accidentally discover that people live within the rock, they are taken prisoner.

The first half of the book involves the discovery of just what is going on in the mysterious caverns, a discovery which the twins make after being befriended by several of the inhabitants —a helicopter pilot, a cultured Chinaman, a doctor, and a tongueless Negro cook. The children sense that none of these individuals particularly likes the Master; and each, for one reason or another, would like to do away with him. However, no one really can subvert him; for he, in his one hundred fifty-seven years, has nearly mastered extrasensory perception—thus, he knows everyone's plottings before they can materialize. Even Dr. McTurk's plan for a *coup d'état* is foiled, and the doctor is sacrificed as an ominous example for anyone else with similar intentions.

The Master himself is not seen very much during the course of the book, but Nicky and Judy know that he plans to conquer the world by rendering all countries powerless with an earth-shaking vibrator which will neutralize all technology. How this machine works is always unspecified, but none on Rockall doubts its efficacy. The Master and his machine remain throughout almost abstract principles and they are unsuited for adventure tales in which young readers would more contentedly read of Long John Silver. In fact, most elements are between the real and the fantastic throughout, and are, therefore, unacceptable either to reality or fantasy and to the reader who desires one or the other. Nicky and Judy are eleven in their actions but not in their speech. The boy quotes Shakespeare continually, for instance, and usually knows the sources of the Master's aphorisms. If either of them is afraid of his precarious position in Rockall, neither displays it as convincingly as Jim Hawkins does in Stevenson's *Treasure Island.* Thus, the reader often gets the sense of being in a cannery rather than atop a dynamo set to paralyze humanity.

Moreover, the rest of the characters themselves are bland and forgettable because of the plot of the story—if our minds are constantly being read by Big Brother, we cannot spare ourselves too many private and revealing thoughts. The Squadron Leader is at all times spineless and unimaginative. The Chinaman's wish to have the Master's power for himself is rather matter-of-fact and unhorrifying. Even the poor cook, whose tongue has been severed merely because he is one person whom the Master cannot control mentally, is the sympathetic victim of tyranny he was meant to be—a Stepin Fetchit, he steps fast to fetch whatever he is told to and never misses his tongue at all. Even the Master himself is not the superman his title implies. He sleeps and drinks too much; and, more than this, he has many of the characteristics of a man one hundred fifty-seven years old. He will probably die soon, knows it, and is, in an attempt to make himself at least partially eternal, looking desperately for a successor. In short, nothing succeeds in this novel.

The most interesting, the most important, and the most destructive sections of the book are those in which the Master's philosophy is debated by his opponents; but even this debate, because two of its participants are eleven years old, is not very Peripatetic. Since the story was initially to be incorporated in *The Once and Future King,* the philosophy requires little outline other than to remark that the discussions are another clash between Might-is-Right and Might-for-Right. Though the Master often sounds like Arthur and Merlyn, he is clearly more worldly and more self-oriented in his ideals than they were. Having control over the entire world has its advantages, as several of the characters point out to one another, since there will be no more war. Yet something nags at the souls of those who are trying to resign themselves to their seemingly certain fate at the Master's hands. What is hard to accept (and, for Nicky, impossible to accept) is the concomitant necessity that the end justifies the means. The Master makes no bones about the fact that several million people will have to die as an example to any who might subsequently rebel and try to overthrow his cosmic government.

The Master obviously believes these deaths are justified; and, through extrasensory perception, he convinces the others when the crucial moment for world conquest finally arrives. All but Nicky are converted, but Nicky has never been beaten by the Master—his mind remains his own. He cannot believe that the end justifies the means; he cannot, in fact, even bring himself to shoot the Master (he would be the only one capable of mental secrecy), despite the fact that he could save millions of lives by doing so. When he finally convinces himself torturously that it *must* be done, his morality overrules him and opens his mind to the Master's suspicious eye. The last chance to stop the plot has failed.

What finally defeats the Master is the same thing that defeats Arthur and Lancelot—his humanity. Where Arthur and Lancelot cannot consistently keep the weaknesses of the flesh in the background, the Master, on the other hand, cannot protect his own weak flesh against *every* threat to his existence. No human mind can beat him; but, as he relishes his impending conquest atop Rockall in the final chapters, he suddenly trips over the twins' dog, Jokey, falls into the sea, and drowns. Thus, just as in the tetralogy, determinism seems the final word—Jokey has been the instrument for the cosmic joke which is played upon all humans, no matter how high or low their aims, simply because they are, in fact, not divine but human. This dualism, so thoroughly investigated in the Arthurian tales, represents the limitless supernatural soul confined in a limited natural body. And, to go one step further, because of this duality no man can profitably rule all other men, no matter how utopian the possibilities might seem: all men are, no matter how hard they try not to be, egocentric; and all men are, no matter how much they refuse to recognize it, mortal.

The Master fails, therefore, in much the same way that *The Queen of Air and Darkness* does: too many unrelated matters are dealt with in too limited space within a too frail framework. Successful novels usually deal with plots and characters which are either fully believable or totally incredible. *The Master* is written for two different audiences (the juvenile and the philosophical) about persons, places and things which are half real, half not—and they are foggy and undynamic. And, once again, White cannot complete a book without the long, irrelevant satire which breaks the unity of so many of his stories—this time a satire on factual presentations by various news media and upon the varying reactions of different countries to global crises. These satires are rather humorously done, but they are, as usual, out of place. *The Master* is a failure from almost every aspect of novelistic artistry.

III The Godstone and the Blackymor

The Godstone and the Blackymor, the last book which White prepared for publication,[5] was originally entitled "Portrait of White as a Confused Person" (a title which would not really have been relevant); and it was eventually published in America as *A Western Wind*. This book is a series of vignettes about people, places, and things White encountered during his residence in Ireland at Belmullet from 1939–40. He assembled the volume in 1958 from diaries kept during his stay, and the book was published in June, 1959. It is nicely illustrated in pencil sketches done by Edward Ardizzone, who felt compelled to visit western Ireland in order to do them.

The Godstone and the Blackymor is most obviously a more rational, though nonetheless critical examination of Ireland and the Irish psyche, than White's previous investigation of the same subject in *The Elephant and the Kangaroo*. By the conclusion of the book, however, White has achieved a new understanding of these curious people, an understanding which causes him to realize that, while they do not possess the social frills and polish of himself and his countrymen, they have an awareness of the ultimate meaning and direction of life that few "sophisticated" Englishmen will ever attain. *The Godstone and the Blackymor* is ultimately, then, the journey of White's soul from cynicism to inspiration.

The first of these dozen vignettes, entitled "Losing a Falcon," is extremely reminiscent of *The Goshawk;* but the story involves a different bird in a different place. Much as Gos did in the earlier book, Cressida, a peregrine, escapes through a careless error on White's part; but this time the discouraged falconer manages to retrieve her the following day by shooting a grouse for her to feast upon. The same intensity of purpose and defensiveness of technique that White demonstrates in *The Goshawk* are once again evident; but, when compared to the greater work, this portrait is too brief to add to the study of White the falconer.

The note of disgust with himself in particular and with human beings in general which concludes the first section is carried directly into the second, "The Blackymor," in which White prejudicially overreacts to a huge Negro he finds sitting one night at his hotel dinner table. Conversing condescendingly and grudgingly, White learns from the man that he is a medicine salesman who travels from country fair to country fair, optimistically seeking out whatever living he can. Certain not only that the man is a fraud but also that his fraudulence does not garner much profit, White tries to do a good deed for both him and his aging, aching friend Dennis Burke. White induces the Negro (who is also a masseur) to give the old man a rub down, hoping to loosen his long-ago-stiffened limbs. After the black man does so, Dennis feels surprisingly better. In order to pay the Negro as little as possible, White leaves his payment with the landlady the night before the blackymor is to leave the area. Even though paid only two pounds, the man leaves a note behind which reads: "Many thanks for the enclosed fee, but honestly I did not expect so much being we are friends" (52). Heretofore misanthropic, White is suddenly both ashamed of himself and happy about the man he had tacitly wronged. This episode is one of the book's more moving and memorable moments.

After an unmemorable reminiscence about his friend Jack, the garage mechanic, and a feeble old man named Desmond to whom Jack devoted much time and sympathy, in the section entitled "The Bird Life," White presents "The Fairy Fire," the first of his investigations of Irish folklore and legend and the beginning of the book's core material. This chapter is, though, more one of infection than investigation; for it contains White's first realization of the effect the atmosphere of an area can have even upon a more sophisticated intruder. After a day of geese hunting, White, Jack, and their young Irish guide are walking through the bog to their car. In the darkness they notice that their footprints emit a phosphorescent glow and that Brownie's circular capering is surrounded them with rings of green fire. At first frightened, White hurries to the car; but, before reaching it, he feels compelled to return to examine the phenomenon. The fire, however, is found to have no sensible qualities except visibility, and White leaves the area concerned and dissatisfied. Since the phenomenon, called "fairy fire," is only an occasional occurrence, the mystery is more puzzling still for the Englishman. He goes to bed that night enveloped in the seemingly credible superstitions of the entire area. He is haunted.

The succeeding chapter, "Letter from a Goose Shooter," is a portrait of White's actively enveloping himself in the superstition of the island. On the pretext of shooting geese in a good goose-shooting location, he lives for three days on a deserted, curse-ridden island off Ireland's northwest coast. On the island of North Inniskea he first hears from two amazed folk from Belmullet (who are amazed that he has survived a night among the local malevolent fairies) about the Godstone, a sacred relic which the people of the South Island long ago had stolen from the people of the North Island. White listens raptly as he hears the folk relate various fantastic stories about the stone's magical powers. To a man who has been stunned by the semi-veracity of much that he has recently encountered and to a man who, on his first night on the island, mistook a roaming black bullock for the Devil, the Godstone is an intriguing concept. Since local legend seems to have lost track of the stone's whereabouts, White is resolved to find it as, on the surface, an anthropological experiment, but as the result really of his newly cultivated theological curiosity.

The following section, the book's fulcrum, is appropriately entitled "The Godstone": "The Godstone had begun to fascinate me. It became a wild goose chase of its own" (95). But the pursuit is destined—because of flaws peculiar both to White and to Ireland—to be in one way a fruitless search: "My heavy mind —too blunt, direct, and Saxon—was bejingled with ideas about paganism and phallic pillars and the claptrap of a half-baked archaeologist" (96). Besides this factor, however, the degree to which the illusive and unpicturable Godstone had become legendary made the object impossible to trace. Despite tireless interviewing of Belmullet's most ancient citizens and despite his surveying of its youngest, most-able-to-recall-rumors schoolchildren, White is unable to obtain even an accurate description of the sacred object, its powers, its guardians, or its supposed destroyers (thought alternately to be pirates grubbing for riches or a priest attempting to loose the area from the chains of superstition). About all White is able to determine is that the stone has a verifiable history, but what the accurate account of it was is anyone's guess. It was thought to have prevented fire and to have controlled the weather—facts that the involved White seems willing enough to accept, if he could find consistent evidence of anything at all. But the entire legend, like all of Ireland, was a problem too irrational to be penetrated, despite the erudition and scholarship he had exerted.

Unfortunately, many of the vignettes in this volume are something less than models of unity and coherence, as is the book itself. With "Snow in Erris," however, the core matter and the structure begin to manifest themselves. Somewhere, beneath the claptrap the world has insisted upon attaching to its various conceptions of God, there seems, for White, to be a Godly Force which, relieved of such superstitions, could be God Himself in the Absolute. *The Godstone and the Blackymor* seems, therefore, to be sifting spiritual plausibility from spiritual thrill-seeking. In "The Godstone" White, by various devices, had attempted to separate the tradition which he had scorned from the realities he has nevertheless continually intuited; and, in "Snow in Erris," he examines the legend of a castrated giant, the Delilah who ruined him, and the ingrate rival who lured his wife away.

The rival, having induced the wife to render the giant vulnerable, repays her by drowning her. Her vengeful soul leaves her body in the shape of a crane and flies to Inniskea, and White immediately connects this incident with rumors of a fated crane all through his studies of the Godstone. Although he is unable to uncover any more about them, the connection of the two stories gives voice to the book's thematic statement concerning the relationship of the real to the legendary:

> You came there with scientific prejudices against fairies and against the claptrap of the Dublin poeticals—and the inhabitants patiently repeated their legends. There really was a Fairy Fire, which I had seen and indeed licked with my own physical tongue. There really was a naomhóg, a minor deity who turned out to be the pillow of a Christian hermit. There really was an island, just as O'Flaherty and indeed Giraldus in the twelfth century had related, where bodies did not decay because of some property in the soil, and where women were not welcome—because it had been a monastery. Here was a vast complex of traditional history, much richer than anything remembered by the English prior to 1066, and something real always seemed to turn up under the legend. (144)

This clarification of theme does not, however, render the remainder of the book beyond reproach. The next piece, "A Love Affair," is little more than a series of random contrasts between the old Ireland and the new which also contain a few reflections about Irish marriage laws and customs—material which seems barely relevant to anything covered earlier.

"A New Boy in the School of Death" is more thematic in that it differentiates between the preposterous accidentals of Irish religion and the more basic and tenaciously held belief that life on earth is a mere preface to the eternal life of the soul after the death of the body. Despite White's skepticism about Ireland and the Irish, he cannot disregard the real purity of thought here. The raucousness of an Irish funeral compared to the over embellishment and grief of death among those less convinced of the truth of the religion in which they "believe" propels White to reveries of guarded praise which he seldom offers the Irish:

> Yet this attitude to death, after the first shock, was not repulsive.
>
> It was the unbelievers who had to cosset their corpses with fireproof vaults of eternal concrete in Hollywood. They had nothing else to tend. For believers—and the peasants of Erris were absolute believers—

> it did not matter much what happened to the body, after the soul had been waked away to Purgatory. They could afford to leave the dry ribs in the rabbit holes nonchalantly, because the important part was under care elsewhere. The Irish Catholic, indeed, with his reliance on the hereafter, always was less concerned about death, bloodshed, war or murder than his English cousin, who secretly doubted the future life. Murder, to a Saxon, was the great sin: it took away the greatest thing he could think of, life. The Catholic Gael regarded murder only as an incident in the existence of the eternal spirit, which could not be destroyed. For him, adultery was the greatest sin, because it was dangerous to salvation. (171)

If the book to this point has concerned itself with the isolated and the physical, the concluding chapters, some of the strongest in the work, are definitely transcendental and metaphysical. "Giving Up Shooting," though mainly about hunting, contains the ever-present White invective against war and the destruction of life. Having discovered a spirit of God which continually manifests itself, whether in fairy fire or in personal dealings with men, White becomes more protective of this manifestation's integrity. The swan he kills in this story on a December morning becomes symbolic of the base human attitude which selfishly destroys anything which will glut its ego, one ever in need of a feeling of superiority, and which forces men into fantastic inversions of the natural order to discover perfection and godliness. White does not give up shooting, but he has suddenly realized the unnatural results of a sport in which he has been a lifelong participant.

The culmination of *The Godstone and the Blackymor* comes in the penultimate chapter, "A Pilgrim Son." In it, White, despite his continuing skepticism about Catholicism—which is still to him an unnatural contrivance by which man replaces the natural path to God which his evil nature is unable to follow—embarks upon a Catholic pilgrimage to the top of a mountain. Like Chaucer, White is overlooking the doctrinal eccentricities which seem to permeate the event (saints and the archbishop's ring); for he is attempting, instead, to absorb the natural human feeling—the feeling of unadulterated love and good will—in an effort to experience the present-but-elusive, transcendent, godly spirit of the universe. Through the efforts of the archbishop, White becomes, not a Catholic, but a man of God in the doctrineless sense. He does not condemn the Catholics, for they are using their religion in much the same way that he himself does. The pilgrimage is guidance for them, and it is a climate or a mood for him. At the top of the mountain, all who follow sincerely in their own beliefs and methods are granted the visions they have come to see. This distinction between the doctrinal Christian and the doctrineless man of God, though clear in retrospect to White the author, is not immediately evident to White the pilgrim: "We went to bed at midnight, replenished with our happy day. I was determined to regularize my spiritual relations with the Archbishop, by being baptized as soon as possible. Of course I never was" (209). He is never able to escape the fact that, for him, organized religion of any variety thwarts an easier, more natural transcendent experience of God. For some, however, especially for those less sensitive or for those less prone to seek (as perhaps White himself was at the book's beginning), organized religion is an admitted necessity.

Whereas *The Elephant and the Kangaroo* ended with an hysterical seeker hysterically haranguing Ireland for all that is wrong with it, *The Godstone and the Blackymor* concludes with "Not Clowns"—a quiet discussion White has with his friend Sean which not only seeks to explain the country's inconsistencies but also to demonstrate its considerable virtues. Boh stem from the same roots: "we *are* innocent and we *are* simple" (213). On the other hand, unlike the Englishman who generally is too blasé to do so, the Irishman responds to the necessities of things higher than himself, often naively and often with too much indirection. For these same reasons, however, the philosophy of life of the Irishman is bound to be different: "'It is absolutely true,' said Sean after a bit, 'that the Irish do set less store on the value of human life than the English do. It may be because their lives are actually harder—less valuable. Also, being Catholics, they don't believe that death mean extinction. Or perhaps it is just a characteristic of the race'" (220).

In this statement the same author who so severely scorned the Irish in several books finally understands the intangible they possess—the realization of Something Greater—which makes them ultimately admirable. Sean speaks in the final pages of the fact that White, at long last, is "being civilized." White, who in an earlier time would have been incensed at such an implication, tacitly but firmly agrees. This book, then, though disunified, recounts White's spiritual awakening.

IV America At Last

America At Last the last book T. H. White ever wrote, was never intended for publication. An inveterate journal keeper, he could not resist the temptation to record the random impressions he had garnered in 1963 and early 1964 during his long-yearned-for trip to the United States. The book was published, however, in America in 1965 (his only book to be published primarily for an American audience) under the guidance of his closest friend David Garnett. By way of introduction Garnett provides a capsule summary of White's life in which he touches fondly upon his happy memories of "Tim" and nudges sympathetically at his shortcomings. In 1965, the introduction was a very short but very intimate sketch—today it is overshadowed by the Sylvia Townsend Warner biography which recounts the Garnett material but adds much more.[7]

On September 19, 1963, White and his eighteen-year-old secretary Carol Walton, a sister-in-law of actress Julie Andrews —an old friend of White's from the *Camelot* days), embarked for New York on the *Queen Elizabeth*. After a whirl of social evenings and of squash playing which had tired White before he arrived, they docked on September 24, after many journal pages which satirize "first class people" (those who travel first class on ships). Initially, White was apprehensive; since he was not a professional lecturer, he feared that he was committing "professional suicide." For a week before the first speech, which was due on the first of October at Williams College, he attempted to lose himself in New York, where he particularly admired the "homely" architecture of Greenwich Village and the "grace" with which the residents of Harlem loped along the streets. However, he castigated America (and also England) for its fantastic devotion to ball games (all he could find one Sunday afternoon on television). As the initial lecture came within two days, he became edgier and more self-pitying—"life is an insoluble pain" (46).

But the talk ("The Pleasures of Learning") at Williams was a success, and this particular college, with its affable students and colonial architecture, becomes for White the pleasant symbol of his entire American experience—indeed, Williams is always mentioned first in his consistent cataloguing of American virtues. On the second of October he continued on to Boston and, though disliking the snobbery of the city itself, was impressed by Old Ironsides, by a Jesuit from Boston College (where White spoke) named Father Sweeney, and, most of all, by the standing ovation he received from the Boston College audience.[9] Such a reception happened once again during his tour, and after each he had the feeling of being a showman rather than an individual hired to bore a captive audience.

From Boston the itinerary zig-zagged around the country, and his audiences varied from those of enormous universities to those of smaller colleges to, occasionally, the smallest clubs. The talks were almost always "The Pleasures of Learning" or about the Roman Emperor Hadrian (with slides). The next stop was Raleigh, North Carolina; then Charlotte; and, at the end of the first ten days of speaking, Washington, D. C. White was tremendously impressed by almost everything in Washington—its original architecture (it was built to be the capital of the greatest country in the world), by the Washington Monument, and most of all by the, for him, all-present aura of Thomas Jefferson, who was to White easily the greatest American in history and a man to whom he pays the ultimate compliment of comparing to his beloved Hadrian. One day, in fact, he and Carol took a three hundred-mile bus trip just to visit Monticello. Two things about Washington which irritated him, however, were the printing of dollar bills,[10] a phenomenon he could not stomach even to observe, and the rather uncosmopolitan way Americans sculpt overly modest nude statues. There are several brief essays on fig leaves throughout the course of *America At Last*. But Washington, which White visited only to see, he found tremendously impressive.

From Washington he went to West Virginia Wesleyan ("what is not a haze is the immense movement toward culture and grace which even these backwoods colleges have achieved" [100–101]) and to Philadelphia, a city he recalled with disfavor because of an argument he had with the sponsors of his lecture over the number of slides to be used in the Hadrian talk. In Buffalo, on October 17, 1963, he experienced an ironic interest in the assassination of President McKinley (which had happened there); and when he viewed Niagara Falls, he felt the artist's Oscar-Wilde-ish disappointment in the entire spectacle. But his lectures were being received in excellent fashion, and White only wished there were more time to see all the things his tight schedule forced him to bypass. When he arrived on the West Coast, he found San Francisco charming, with the exception of Fisherman's Wharf (a joke). His lecture, given at the Curran Theater, was one of his more difficult because of a series of mishaps. From San Francisco, he went to Los Angeles.

Within four days he had spoken at Southern California, the University of Las Vegas (for White, Las Vegas was the supreme symbol of American innocence—but still a nice place to live and to teach), and UCLA (though he was feeling sick before his performance, it was his best audience since Boston).

To know that White was to die only one month after his last entry in his American journal is to render its tone of exuberant happiness all the more tragic. White, in none of his later books, seemed so glad to be alive or so tolerant of diversity and adversity as he is here. At first, he is prone to display a "typically English" reaction to American culture (or lack of it); but White, before a day on American soil ends, is charmed by its ingenuousness. America, he finds, is young and innocent; but, though making mistakes, it is destined for greater achievements than its parent country was ever capable of attaining. Having been confined to a New Orleans hospital from exhaustion two months after his arrival, White, five days after the assassination of President Kennedy, finally has a free moment to reflect upon the American character:

> Adolescent America. Of course I am writing of the average, not of the intellectual—who is as international as anybody else. The average person is simple, religious, modest if not puritan about sex, proud of

his nation and particularly of his own birthplace, uncultured but respectful to culture, anxious as any other adolescent to be admired for being right, essentially good, benevolent, sentimental, prone like the young to outbursts, not very intelligent, dedicated to the herd, obtuse about variants, vigorous, in short like most other average schoolboys. He has a hard side of obstinate intolerance which comes out in witch hunts—most adolescents want to "belong" to clubs or societies—Ku Klux Klans—and he is uncertain about the difference between right and wrong, uncertain whether he is being "correct." (214–15)[8]

This statement is White's most complete one of his impression of the American character—the result of two months of notetaking in every part of the country. At the outset of the trip, wondering if the diary was worth keeping at all since millions of people have visited America, White states his thesis for *America At Last* in particular (and for his trip in general):

So why not write a book as we go? It would keep us observant, not be too much trouble for a short entry every day, and at least it could do no harm. Also, it would be a distraction in all those hundreds and thousands of miles by terrifying airplanes.
QUERY: Does it do harm to write needless books? "Of the making of books there is no end." Why write if you have nothing to write about? Is one trip round America sufficient excuse? Millions do it.
I suppose it is excusable, if you keep your eyes wide open. (19–20)

During the next three months, White, between delivering the lectures he had come to America to give and absorbing everything America had to offer in return, wanted, though exhausted, the trip never to end.

One of the most interesting things about *America At Last* is the manner in which White introduces common American topics for detached discussion at appropriate times. When speaking in North Carolina, White wrote in his journal of the race problems in America; and he indicates that he was not unwilling to consider the Southern side of the question. In Los Angeles, America's fastest growing city, White speaks, not unpoetically, of urban blight:

Los Angeles is suffering the transition that happened to Buffalo and that seems usual in American cities. They grow outwards from the center, which decays into a slum, and finally the tycoons of the periphery repurchase the middle bit and erect their civic center on it with great magnificence.

This re-erection has not yet been completed in L.A., with result that the poor man's plain is still unprepossessing and apparently interminable. (130–31)

If *America At Last* anywhere lacks taste, it is in the discussion of Walt Disney, which recurs many times in the second half of the book, but is initiated on the day (October 26) that White visited Disneyland. Disney is severely attacked, and it is hard not to believe that the invective was due to the fact that Disney had purchased some twenty-five years earlier the film rights to *The Sword in the Stone* for a piddling sum. As for Disney, White observes that "Chaucer believed that animals must be true to themselves. He praised a horse for being 'right horsely.' Disney's horses are not, his mermaids are not mermaidly nor his sea serpents sepentine—nor are his humans human. For one thing, they are completely sexless—which, so far as I can see, cuts out about 80% of human life" (142).

White, as we know, was never a child—and maybe this fact accounts for his lack of sympathy for something artistic in a way far different from White's concept of the term. With equally poor logic, he later compares Disneyland with the colony established by Brigham Young: "I said that Disneyland came out of the brain of one man. What a mouse's fart it seems beside the whole of Utah, which came out of the brain of Brigham Young" (186).

As the tour continues in the Northwest, White, as usual, sifts good from bad as he travels; but Western movies and American attitudes toward homosexuality ("as much a bugbear as communism is" [167]) bear the brunt of the attacks. Salt Lake City and the Mormon struggle for survival are praised effusively. From here he went to Chicago (where he sees "How the West Was Won"—an epic of human endurance); Jacksonville, Illinois (a sparse audience at MacMurray College because of incorrect publicity); Pittsburgh (sees a road company of *Camelot*); Columbus (finds it hard to deceive an adult audience at the Crichton Club); Delaware, Ohio (at Ohio Wesleyan he learns of panty raids and other fraternity practices); and New

Orleans (after a jarring four-plane trip). On the day after arriving in New Orleans, his diary breaks off—he had collapsed of exhaustion.

The next entry in the journal has a fateful date attached to it —November 22, 1963; and, writing in bed, White penned his apostrophe to President John Kennedy:

> Born to enormous riches, educated at Harvard (where he was a pretty good swimmer), allowed as a Harvard junior to come down here to New Orleans for the thrill of the Mardi Gras, amorous, lucky and courageous in war, dedicated by his unpopular father to public life because an elder brother was dead or else bitten by the bug of public speaking as I have tardily been, astonishingly selected to perhaps the most powerful public office in the world, faced by fearsome decisions involving atomic war, hated by the Deep South, educated as a statesman while he went along (the youngest U. S. President), physically handicapped by spinal injury, rumored to be prepotent, spotlighted by day and night, a guard on his lips where none could really guard his life, never not the jeune premier, one of the three most important people in the world, and now murdered eleven years younger than I am—his birthday was the same day as mine—did he really think he was making History or being made by it? What would his answer have been to Tolstoy, who thought that Napoleon was the slave of France and not her master? Did he think it had been worth it? Was he happy? How would he have gotten on with my emperor Hadrian?
>
> I wonder what Madame Nhu is thinking about? What do great people think about? What does God think about? (210–11)

White, released from the hospital on December 1, 1963, spoke during the next two weeks in Washington, New York, Wilmington, Delaware, and Philadelphia. The tour ended in such a blaze of happiness for both him and Carol that the final lecture (in Philadelphia on December 16) caused White to write near the end of his American journal "I don't want to stop ever ever ever" (247). But, at this point, the American tour had somewhat tragically ended—and, within a month and a day, very tragically, so had White's life. The death of T. H. White occurred on January 17, 1964, on board the S.S. *Exeter* in the port of Piraeus (Athens), Greece, of a heart attack at the age of fifty-seven; but this is not a proper topic here.

America At Last is the self-portrait of a man who was at the end of his life more alive than he had ever before allowed himself to be. And America seemingly forced him, despite himself, to recover so much vitality, an America which he judged with loving criticism. Perhaps one of his final statements about America in this volume is one of the most telling: "If somebody strikes against it [America], as happened at Pearl Harbor, they will always react with a blind devastating energy. Americans are more likely to let off an atomic bomb than the Russians are. They are less old, less effete wtih history, more bred from strength, younger, more lovable, more terrible potentially" (236–37). It is difficult to believe that his death came a year before the beginning of all-out warfare in Vietnam.

Conclusion

THE opening chapter of this study attempted to focus White's perspective on life, but a final estimation of his contribution as a creative writer has been withheld. In every White book we find some distinct element which makes it unmistakably his, but that element is elusive when we must ultimately define it. The best estimation of his approach to life seems to me to have been presented in his own words in the sadness-learning statement by Merlyn[11] and in the portrait of Lord Camelford.[12] White was a homosexual who was determined not to foist his problem upon others; thus, he became a semirecluse who tried to manufacture for himself entertaining diversions, but every diversion was permeated by the loneliness and fatalism which continually tried to gain control of his existence.

For this reason, a White book—be it prose, fiction, poetry, or whatever—usually possesses a dualism between surface and subsurface. A work at first appears to be lilting and fabulistic, but this characteristic is invariably a masque for the sombre and reflective countenance which always lurks behind. And this masque, as Sylvia Warner has stated, always has painted on it a pair of raised-eyebrows, for White's tone is continually that of a man who is not surprised by what he sees in life but is rather insistently critical of it. The criticism is generally delivered lightly, with a pointed finger rather than with an upraised switch. If his eyebrows are raised, his voice accompanies them with a "tsk-tsk" of forced indignation.

In an attempt to be a Camelford superman in his literature to offset what he felt to be substantial weaknesses of character, White was a very versatile and original writer at his best—and very stodgy and imitative at his worst. Never a great creator of realistic characters, his finest work is that in which he sets characterization aside in favor of humor, satire, fantasy, and amateur philosophizing. Beyond fiction, his own life was interesting and dynamic to a degree that even one of his daybooks makes good reading. But when White tried to write poetry, Gerard Manley Hopkins seemed to be a model he could neither duplicate nor avoid. Likewise, in his early fiction, the influence of Conan Doyle, Aldous Huxley, Evelyn Waugh and others is much too obvious.

White, in fact, never was able to steer clear of another author's work in creating his own. In his early years, he imitated and failed; in his later ones, he extended and spoofed and, consequently, succeeded. Malory, Swift, Horace Walpole, and Stevenson all retire far into the background when White is delving into their respective milieus. As a scholar, White is interesting and entertaining but probably not lasting, for he could never dispel a sense of dabbling and dilettantism for himself or his readers.

So T. H. White is important to English Literature mainly as a novelist and a diarist. *Farewell Victoria, The Once and Future King, Mistress Masham's Repose, The Elephant and the Kangaroo* are certainly the finest examples of the White style; for they contain the most compelling combination of fantasy, satire, humor, and philosophical reflection. They are the books in which the eyebrows are raised the highest and in which the determination to make life worthwhile, despite the odds against doing so, is the strongest. None of these works could be called "modern" British fiction, but all of them are important and memorable contributions by a fine British writer.

As a diarist, White's own dominating personality, his fear of the unknown, his determination to overcome that fear, the endeavors through which he does so, and the musings upon the actual course of life as he knows it magnetize these themes together and universalize them. *England Have My Bones, The Goshawk, The Godstone and the Blackymor*, and *America At Last* are unique in the canon of English Literature. They are the type of book written about deceased authors by intimate acquaintances, but these works possess the intimacy of the man himself as he lived them and realized them. In this particular genre, whatever one chooses to call it, White probably has no equal. Hemingway's *A Moveable Feast* and Mailer's *Armies of the Night* are the only books which seem to me to be even close to White's.

T. H. White was a man who despised life as it was made for him by his mother, his homosexuality, organized religion, and world politics. Yet, by receding within himself and speaking to the world from this hideaway, he was—like Mundy, Merlyn, the Professor at Malplaquet, Mr. White of Burkestown, and Tim White of the journals—able to fashion his life into a meaningful existence in which his own standards and personal morality replaced those which would otherwise have been imposed upon him by the modern world's manufactured machinery, manufactured war, manufactured god, and manufactured Hell.

Notes and References

Chapter One

1. John Verney, in his Foreword to the Sylvia Warner biography, recounts an occasion in Italy when an American woman approached White, seeking the autograph of Ernest Hemingway.

2. The biographers of the two men, Carlos Baker and Sylvia Warner, provide stories in which both became highly incensed when others proved more proficient than they.

3. The inscription on White's tomb reads: "*T. H. White*, 1906–1964, Author, Who from Troubled Heart Delighted Others Loving and Praising This Life."

4. Sylvia Townsend Warner, *T. H. White: A Biography* (London, 1967).

5. David Garnett, ed., *The White/Garnett Letters* (London, 1968).

6. Warner, *T. H. White*, p. 28.

7. White was forced to move to the Channel Island of Alderney in 1946 because both the United States and Great Britain were imposing income taxes upon the profits from his books.

8. *The Once and Future King* (London, 1958), pp. 185–86. This quotation is also reproduced in this volume (Chapter 4, p. 00).

9. Warner, *T. H. White*, pp. 265–99.

10. The friendship with Potts lasted from 1925, when he became White's tutor at Cambridge, until his death in 1960. David Garnett reviewed the Aston book, *They Winter Abroad*, and became a constant correspondent of White's from 1936 onward when the author solicited his opinion of *England Have My Bones*. White met Cockerell in 1938 when he was invited to examine the collector's prized books in his personal library.

11. These years are beautifully recounted in *The Goshawk* (London, 1951) and *England Have My Bones* (London, 1936).

12. The Broadway musical *Camelot* is, of course, based upon various parts of *The Once and Future King*. Lerner and Loewe paid White a figure in the vicinity of $400,000 for stage rights to the novel.

Chapter Two

1. *Loved Helen and Other Poems* (London, 1929). All page numbers refer to the Chatto and Windus edition.

2. The T. H. White who became famous does not, it seems to me, make an appearance until *Farewell Victoria* in 1933.

3. In addition to the critical study of Hopkins that White undertook, the poet is referred to in many of White's books, such as *Farewell Victoria, America at Last,* and others.

4. Warner, *T. H. White*, p. 50.

5. W. H. Gardner and N. H. MacKenzie (eds.), *The Poems of Gerard Manley Hopkins* (Oxford, 1967), p. 99. Quotations from *The Green Bay Tree* by White are from the pamphlet issued by Heffer in 1929, Number 3, in the series "Songs for Sixpence."

6. Warner, *T. H. White*, p. 52.

7. T. H. White and R. McNair Scott, *Dead Mr. Nixon* (London, 1931). All page numbers refer to the Cassell edition.

8. Warner, *T. H. White*, p. 52.

9. Cf. "The Man of Law's Tale" in *The Canterbury Tales.*

10. James Aston [T. H. White], *They Winter Abroad* (New York, 1932). Page reference is to the American edition by Viking.

11. James Aston [T. H. White], *First Lesson* (New York, 1933). All page numbers refer to the American edition by Alfred A. Knopf, Inc.

12. Dante, *Il Paradiso*, Canto 33, ll. 142–45.

13. Warner, *T. H. White*, p. 52. Her apparent lack of femininity was, as White's biographer sagely points out, probably due to the fact that *First Lesson* was originally to be a novel of homosexual love.

Chapter Three

1. T. H. White, *Farewell Victoria* (New York, 1934). All page numbers refer to the American edition by Smith and Haas.

2. All quotations from reviews have been gathered from the dust-jacket Collins placed on the original edition of *Farewell Victoria.*

3. Warner, *T. H. White*, p. 79.

4. Cf. especially *Burke's Steerage* and *The Sword in the Stone.*

5. *Earth Stopped* (London, 1934). All page numbers refer to the Collins edition.

6. *They Winter Abroad* in 1932.

7. *New Statesman*, March 7, 1936.

8. Quoted on the jacket of the Collins edition.

9. *England Have My Bones* (London, 1936). All page numbers refer to the Collins edition.

10. Cf. *The Goshawk* (1951), *The Godstone and the Blackymor* (1959), *America at Last* (1965).

11. Warner, *T. H. White*, p. 194.

12. Cf. n. 8 above.

13. Letter of White to L. J. Potts, January 14, 1938.

14. The title, of course, is a satiric variation upon John Burke's *A Genealogical and Heraldic History of the Peerage and Baronetage of the United Kingdom* (1826) and published annually since 1847 under its popular title, *Burke's Peerage.*

15. *Burke's Steerage* (London, 1938). All page numbers refer to the Collins edition.

Chapter Four

1. One problem which is present throughout the tetralogy but which White seldom speaks of directly is the difficult position Merlyn is in when, in training Arthur, he is actually trying to reverse fate but, since he lives backwards in time, knows what will of necessity happen because it has already happened for him.

2. *The Sword in the Stone*, in *The Once and Future King*, pp. 1–213. All page numbers refer to those in the tetralogy issued by Collins rather than to the single novel published in 1938.

3. In Chapter 11 only young people can rescue the prisoners from Morgan Le Fay's griffin, for older people would immediately, according to Robin Wood, succumb to the pleasures of the castle.

4. Cf. *The Ill-Made Knight.*

5. To name several, the Professor in *Mistress Masham's Repose*, the Master, Mr. White in *The Elephant and the Kangaroo.*

6. Brownie, the only being White seems really to have loved, was with White from 1933–44. However, she had periods of severe illness and nearly died several times. On another occasion White, thinking he would have to go to war, began phasing Brownie out of his life, lest the ultimate split ruin both of them. White never went, and Brownie was one of the reasons. The whole relationship with her, however, was darkened by the fear, real and invented, that he had of losing her.

7. *Burke's Steerage, Earth Stopped, England Have My Bones, The Godstone and the Blackymor, America at Last.*

8. *The Queen of Air and Darkness [The Witch in the Wood]*, in *The Once and Future King*, pp. 215–323. Page numbers are handled as in n. 2 above.

9. Perhaps the most important theme in the entire tetralogy is the legality and morality of warfare, though sometimes issues fundamental to the ultimate waging of war dominate the forefront (as in *The Sword in the Stone*) rather than war itself.

10. Cf. Warner, *T. H. White*, chapters 5–7.

11. Unlikely Malory, who sets the struggle with the Gaels straight

from the outset, White totally ignores the question in *The Sword in the Stone.*

12. Perhaps Merlyn, more than in the previous novel, is resigned to accepting the fate he knows will eventuate.

13. Warner, *T. H. White,* p. 123.

14. *Ibid.,* p. 124.

15. The symbolism of the North as a place of evil mystery stems from medieval mythology and folklore. Chaucer's Reeve, who was from the North, was dressed to resemble Death on the pilgrimage.

16. *The Ill-Made Knight,* in *The Once and Future King,* pp. 325–544. Page numbers are handled as in n. 2 above.

17. The definitive consideration of this concept is in D. W. Robertson, *A Preface to Chaucer: Studies in Medieval Perspectives* (Princeton, N. J., 1963).

18. *The Candle in the Wind* was not published until 1958, but it is discussed here in order to complete the unity of the tetralogy.

19. *The Candle in the Wind,* in *The Once and Future King,* pp. 545–677. Page numbers are handled as in n. 2 above.

Chapter Five

1. Warner, *T. H. White,* p. 216. This paraphrase (by Warner) of the original letter, dated Easter Sunday, 1945, is from Garnett to White. For the full text, full of help and criticism, some of which White accepted, see Garnett, *The White/Garnett Letters,* pp. 192–93.

2. Jonathan Swift, *Gulliver's Travels,* Part I, Chapter 8.

3. *Mistress Masham's Repose* (London, 1947). All page numbers refer to the Jonathan Cape edition.

4. Cf. *The Goshawk,* the "Scandal" books, the Arthurian tetralogy and others.

5. Warner, *T. H. White,* p. 199.

6. Originally to have been the "Holy Ghost" but recommended against by Garnett. Cf. Garnett, *The White/Garnett Letters,* pp. 189–91.

7. T. H. White, *The Elephant and the Kangaroo* (London, 1948). All page numbers refer to the Jonathan Cape edition.

8. White, when met at the airport in Boston in 1963 by two Jesuit priests, remarked that he had once almost become a Catholic; but in the long run he had discovered that he didn't believe a word of it. For the details of White's near-conversion see pages 120–65 in the Warner biography.

9. *The Age of Scandal* (New York, 1950). All page numbers refer to the edition published by G. P. Putnam's Sons.

10. Cf. Pope's "Epistle to Dr. Arbuthnot," ll. 305–33.

11. Actually *The Goshawk*'s publication intervened between the two "Scandal" books, but the order of consideration has been altered in the discussion in favor of unity.

12. Warner, *T. H. White*, pp. 245–46.

13. Cf. this study, Chapter 1, n. 8.

14. *The Scandalmonger* (New York, 1952). All page numbers refer to the edition published by G. P. Putnam's Sons.

15. *The Goshawk* (New York, 1952). All page numbers refer to the edition published by G. P. Putnam's Sons.

16. See page 244 in the Warner biography for Garnett's opinion of the book that he submitted in its support to Cape.

17. Cf. the first paragraph of this section.

18. Cf. William Wordsworth, "Tintern Abbey," l. 46.

19. Of which *The Goshawk*, though not published then, was one.

Chapter Six

1. Other results of the same desire are *The Age of Scandal*, *The Scandalmonger*, and *The Godstone and the Blackymor*.

2. Quoted from a letter to L. J. Potts, February 18, 1944, which is reproduced in the Warner biography, p. 202.

3. This concept of *sapientia* connects with the discussion of *caritas* in the present consideration of *The Ill-Made Knight* (q.v.). Cf. also Chapter 4, n. 17.

4. *The Bestiary: A Book of Beasts* (New York, 1955). All page numbers refer to the edition published by G. P. Putnam's Sons.

5. The last book, *America at Last*, was prepared by David Garnett from White's American diary. The publication of *The Candle in the Wind* intervened between *The Master* and the present book, but it is considered in Chapter 4 with the other three books of the Arthurian tetralogy.

6. *The Godstone and the Blackymor [A Western Wind]* (London, 1959). All page numbers refer to the edition published by Jonathan Cape.

7. As does also Garnett's own edition of his correspondence with White. Cf. Chapter 1, n. 5.

8. *America at Last*, edited with an introduction by David Garnett (New York, 1965). All page numbers refer to the edition published by G. P. Putnam's Sons.

9. Cf. pp. 59ff.

10. See the picture in the Warner biography, facing p. 273.

11. Cf. Chapter 1, n. 8.

12. Cf. *The Scandalmonger*, pp. 25–26. Also reproduced in this study in Chapter 5, p. 000.

Selected Bibliography

PRIMARY SOURCES

1. Novels

Dead Mr. Nixon. (Written in collaboration with R. McNair Scott.) London: Cassell, 1931.

Darkness at Pemberley. London: Gollancz, 1932; New York: G. P. Putnam's Sons, 1933.

They Winter Abroad. (Written under pseudonym of James Aston.) London: Chatto & Windus, 1932; New York: Viking Press, 1932.

First Lesson. (Written under pseudonym of James Aston.) London: Chatto & Windus, 1932; New York: Alfred A. Knopf, Inc., 1933.

Farewell Victoria. London: Collins, 1933; New York: Smith and Haas, 1934. (Reissued by Jonathan Cape and G. P. Putnam's Sons, 1960.)

Earth Stopped. London: Collins, 1934.

Gone to Ground. London: Collins, 1935.

The Sword in the Stone. London: Collins, 1938; New York: G. P. Putnam's Sons, 1939.

The Witch in the Wood. (In 1958 retitled *The Queen of Air and Darkness.*) New York: G. P. Putnam's Sons, 1939; London: Collins, 1940.

The Ill-Made Knight. New York: G. P. Putnam's Sons, 1940; London: Collins, 1941.

Mistress Masham's Repose. New York: G. P. Putnam's Sons, 1946; London: Jonathan Cape, 1947.

The Elephant and the Kangaroo. New York: G. P. Putnam's Sons, 1947; London: Jonathan Cape, 1948.

The Master: An Adventure Story. London: Jonathan Cape, 1957; New York: G. P. Putnam's Sons, 1957.

The Once and Future King. (Contains *The Sword in the Stone; The Queen of Air and Darkness* [previously entitled *The Witch in the Wood*]; *The Ill-Made Knight*; and *The Candle in the Wind* [previously unpublished].) London: Collins, 1958; New York: G. P. Putnam's Sons, 1958.

2. Journals

England Have My Bones. London: Collins, 1936; New York, Macmillan, 1936.

The Goshawk. London: Jonathan Cape, 1951; New York: G. P. Putnam's Sons, 1952.

The Godstone and the Blackymor. (In America entitled *A Western Wind*.) London: Jonathan Cape, 1959; New York: G. P. Putnam's Sons, 1959.

America at Last. Edited with an Introduction by David Garnett. New York: G. P. Putnam's Sons, 1959.

3. Poetry

Loved Helen and Other Poems. London: Chatto & Windus, 1929; New York: Viking Press, 1929.

The Green Bay Tree; or, Wicked Man Touches Wood. Songs for Six-pence, No. 3. Cambridge: Heffer, 1929.

4. Scholarly Works

The Age of Scandal. London: Jonathan Cape, 1950; New York: G. P. Putnam's Sons, 1950.

The Scandalmonger. London: Jonathan Cape, 1952; New York: G. P. Putnam's Sons, 1952.

The Bestiary: A Book of Beasts. London: Jonathan Cape, 1954; New York: G. P. Putnam's Sons, 1955.

5. Satiric Essay

Burke's Steerage. London: Collins, 1938.

6. Letters

The White/Garnett Letters. Edited by David Garnett. London: Jonathan Cape, 1968.

SECONDARY SOURCES

1. Biography

WARNER, SYLVIA TOWNSEND. *T. H. White: A Biography*. London: Jonathan Cape and Chatto & Windus, 1967; New York: Viking Press, 1968. The only biography available and an excellent one. Especially heavy concentration on the 1930's and 1940's; skimpier before and after.

2. Articles

CAMERON, J. R. "T. H. White in Camelot: The Matter of Britain Revitalized," *Humanities Association Bulletin*, XVI (1965), i, 45–48. The author refers to White as "the major interpreter of the Arthurian legend in the twentieth century," and attempts to place the tetralogy more firmly in the Arthurian tradition.

FLOYD, BARBARA. "A Critique of T. H. White's *The Once and Future King*," *Riverside Quarterly*, I (1965), 175–80; II (1966), 54–57, 127–33, 210–13. Heretofore the only scholarly consideration of the complete tetralogy, these articles consider, in a general way, each of the four novels in turn.

HUGH-JONES, SIRIOL. "A Visible Export: T. H. White, Merlyn's Latest Pupil," *Times Literary Supplement*, August 7, 1969, p. ix. Essentially a review of *The Once and Future King* but discusses the extent to which White built himself into the character of Merlyn.

IRWIN, W. R. "Swift and the Novelists," *Philological Quarterly*, XLV (1966), 102–13. Discussion of two twentieth-century novels, White's *Mistress Masham's Repose* and Walter de la Mare's *Memoirs of a Midget*, which derive their basic materials from *Gulliver's Travels*.

LOTT, HERSHEL W. "The Social and Political Ideals in the Major Writings of T. H. White," *Dissertations Abstracts International* XXXI (1971); 4126A–27A. Sees White as a social critic who finds no political system—totalitarianism, communism, democracy—workable, for all will fall victim to the internal moral decay of individuals.

WEST, RICHARD C. "Contemporary Medieval Authors," *Orcrist* III (1969): 9–10, 15. A discussion of White and Tolkien.

Index

Agate, James, 66, 69
Ananda, 27
Andrews, Julie, 20, 179
Anglo-Saxon Poetic Record, 164
Ardizzone, Edward, 172
Aston, James (pseudonym for T. H. White), 41, 42, 46, 47
Atlas, 27
Augustine of Hippo, 102, 166
Austen, Jane: *Pride and Prejudice,* 37

Beckford, William, 146
Bible, 22
Black Death, 56
Blaine, Gilbert, 154
Boccaccio, Giovanni: *Decameron,* 63
Boer War, 52, 54, 55, 56, 57
Book Society, 22
Boston College, 180
Boswell, James, 146
Browne, Sir Thomas: *Pseudodoxia Epidemica,* 164
Brownie, 18, 20, 84, 84n6, 123, 134, 142, 163, 174
Brummel, Beau, 148, 149-50
Buddha, 28
Burke, John, 70n14
Burn, Johnny, 66, 67
Burney, Fanny, 144, 150
Burton, Richard, 20
Byng, Admiral John, 147
Byron, George Gordon, Lord, 152

Camelford, Lord, 148, 149, 152, 186
Camelot (Broadway Musical), 20, 20n12, 179, 183
Caroline, Queen (wife of George II), 144, 146
Charles II, King, 64
Chatto and Windus (publishers), 47
Chaucer, Geoffrey, 44, 83, 103, 177, 183; *The Canterbury Tales,* 96-n15, 103
Chesterfield, Philip Stanhope, 4th Earl of, 144
Christ, Jesus, 27, 45, 110, 165, 166, 167
Cockerell, Sidney, 20, 20n10
Collins (publishers), 86, 92
Comitatus, 80
Conrad, Joseph: *Nostromo,* 37, 51
Crane, Stephen: *The Red Badge of Courage,* 55, 56
Crichton Club, 183

Daily Mail, 59
Dante Alighieri, 48, 49, 50; *Inferno,* 48
Darwin, Charles, 169
d'Eon, Chevalier, 152
deSade, Marquis, 146, 147
Disney, Walt, 77, 183
Dobbie, Elliot Van Kirk, 164
Dostoevsky, Fyodor, 149
Doyle, Arthur Conan, 187

Edward VII, King, 54
Eliot, T. S., 28; "The Love Song of J. Alfred Prufrock," 24, 54
Emerson, Ralph Waldo, 81
Encyclopedia Britannica, 76

Fascism, 91
Faulkner, William, 51; *Pylon,* 66
Fetchit, Stepin, 170
Frazer, Sir James, 163

Garnett, Amaryllis, 123, 133

Garnett, David, 18, 20, 20n10, 42, 65, 123, 126, 142, 179
George I, King, 144
George II, King, 144
George III, King, 144
George IV, King, 144
Gray, Thomas, 152
Greene, Graham, 59
Grub Street, 147

Hadrian, 180, 184
Helen of Troy, 22
Hemingway, Ernest, 17, 19; *A Farewell to Arms,* 55; *A Moveable Feast,* 187
Hercules, 27
Hervey, John, 142, 144, 145
Hitler, Adolph, 80, 82, 88, 90, 91, 159
Hopkins, Gerard Manley, 28, 29, 31, 187; "The Wreck of the Deutschland," 55
Horace, 80
Howard, Wren, 154
Huxley, Aldous, 42, 45, 187

Jacob, 166
James, M. R., 164
Jefferson, Thomas, 180
Johnson, Samuel, 143, 145, 146, 147, 153, 167
Jonathan Cape (publishers), 86, 154
Juvenal, 80, 123

Keats, John, 23

Las Vegas, University of, 181
Lewis, Matthew "Monk," 146
London Times, 59

McKinley, President William, 181
MacMurray College, 183
Mailer, Norman: *Armies of the Night,* 187
Malory, Thomas, 75, 77, 87, 96, 101, 102, 187
Mandeville, Sir John, 164
Mann, Sir Horace, 147
Mantle, Mickey, 101
Marx, Karl: *Das Kapital,* 60
Melville, Herman, 51; *Moby Dick,* 115

Napoleon, 184
Neoplatonism, 102
Newcastle, Thomas Pelham Holles, Duke of, 147
New Statesman and Nation, 42, 65
Nhu, Madame, 184
Nichol, John, 150
Noah, 141
Norman Conquest, 56

Observer, The, 59
Oedipus, 94, 96
Ohio Wesleyan, 183

Palagonia, Prince of, 150
Pan, 65
Paris (Helen's Lover), 22
Physiologus, 164
Polo, Marco, 164
Pope, Alexander, 142, 145
Porson, Richard, 153
Potts, L. J., 20, 20n10, 38, 86

Queensbury, Duke of, 152

Roxburghe Bestiary, 164, 168

Sassoon, Siegfried, 59
Saturn, 30
Scott, R. McNair, 31, 37
Selwym, George, 146, 153
Shakespeare, William, 22, 107, 156, 161, 170
Shelley, Mary: *Frankenstein,* 152
Shelley, P. B., 152, 161; "Ozymandias," 27
Sheridan, Richard, 150
Song of Songs, 166
Southern California, University of, 181
Spectator, The, 59

Sterne, Laurence: *Tristram Shandy,* 133
Stevenson, Robert Louis: *Treasure Island,* 169, 170, 187
Strachey, Lytton, 22
Sweeney, Father, 180
Swift, Johathan, 64, 77, 123, 187; *Gulliver's Travels,* 124, 125, 126, 128, 130, 131, 132

Thomas, Dylan, 28
Thoreau, Henry David, 81, 159, 160
Tieresias, 96
Tolstoy, Leo, 181
Treatise of Hawks and Hawking, 154
Turberville, George, 159

UCLA, 181

Victoria, Queen, 52, 53, 56, 58, 150
Voltaire, 147

Wagner, Richard, 161
Walpole, Horace, 141, 142, 144, 145, 146, 187
Walpole, Robert, 145
Walton, Carol, 179, 180, 184
Warner, Sylvia Townsend: *T. H. White: A Biography,* 18, 19, 21, 31, 38, 50, 52, 59, 61, 68, 134, 157, 179, 186
Washington, George, 153
Waugh, Evelyn, 187
West Virginia Wesleyan University, 180
White, Constance Aston, 18, 22, 86, 92, 93, 188
White, Garrick, 18
White, Terence Hanbury:

WORKS: FICTION
Book of Merlyn, The (unwritten novel), 79, 168
Candle in the Wind, The, 111, *112-22*
Darkness at Pemberley, 31, *37-42*
Dead Mr. Nixon, 31-37, 47, 50, 51
Earth Stopped, 21, *58-62*
Elephant and the Kangaroo, The, 21, 68, 85, 98, 133, *134-41,* 161, 172, 178, 187
Farewell Victoria, 21, 31, 42, 51, *52-58,* 187
First Lesson, 21, 31, 42, *46-51*
Gone to Ground, 21, *62-65*
Ill-Made Knight, The, 41, 86, *99-112,* 115
Master, The, 41, *168-72*
Mistress Masham's Repose, 21, 41, 50, *123-34,* 187
Once and Future King, The, 18, 20n12, 21, *75-122,* 137, 161, 168, 170, 187
Queen of Air and Darkness, The, 85-99, 107, 108, 114, 172
Sword in the Stone, The, 19, *75-85,* 96, 107, 112, 132, 148, 183
They Winter Abroad, 21, *42-46*
Western Wind, A. See The Godstone and the Blackymor.
Witch in the Wood, The. See The Queen of Air and Darkness.

WORKS: JOURNALS
America at Last, 21, 153, *179-85,* 187
England Have My Bones, 21, *65-70,* 84, 187
Godstone and the Blackymor, The, 21, 85, 98, 123, 141, *172-79,* 187
Goshawk, The, 21, 50, 69, 132, *153-62,* 173, 187

WORKS: POETRY
Green Bay Tree; or, Wicked Man Touches Wood, The, 21, *29-31*
Loved Helen, and Other Poems, 21, *22-28*

WORKS: SCHOLARLY AND SATIRIC
Age of Scandal, The, 21, *141-48,* 150, 152, 161, 164
Bestiary: A Book of Beasts, The, 21, 128, 142, *163-68*
Burke's Steerage, 65, *70-74*

Scandalmonger, The, 21, 142, 145, *148-53,* 161, 164

WORKS: LECTURES
"Hadrian," 180
"Pleasures of Learning, The," 19, 180

Whitman, Walt, 28
Wilde, Oscar, 181
William IV, King, 144
Williams College, 179, 180
William the Conqueror, 77
Woolf, Virginia: *Mrs. Dalloway,* 37
Wordsworth, William, 29, 142; "Tintern Abbey," 160; "The Prelude," 160
World War I, 52
World War II, 19, 90

Yeats, W. B., 28
Young, Brigham, 183

Zed, 18, 20